SCOTS LAW
TERMS AND
EXPRESSIONS

JOHN ANGUS BEATON
C.B., B.L., Solicitor

Formerly Deputy Solicitor to the Secretary of State for Scotland and Director of the Scottish Courts Administration

W. GREEN & SON LTD.
EDINBURGH
1982

First published   1982

© 1982 W. Green & Son Ltd.

ISBN 0 414 00691 7

Printed by Lindsay & Co. Ltd.
16 Orwell Terrace
Edinburgh, EH11 2EU

SCOTS LAW
TERMS AND EXPRESSIONS

PREFACE

The primary purpose of this publication is to give an exposition for the layman of the legal terms (including phrases and expressions) in most frequent use in Scots law at the present time. It also contains references to Scottish legal terms which are not much used currently but, if used, are likely to cause puzzlement and one or two English terms which tend to be used improperly as if they had significance in the Scottish Legal Syetem.

Many of the terms have been suggested for inclusion by those who have seen a draft of the publication and of the S.A.C.A.B. *Glossary of Scottish Legal Terms* which was written by the author of this publication and which forms its foundation although with substantial additions and amendments that, it is hoped, will enable it to fulfil its purpose more readily. The author is grateful to the C.A.B. and particularly to Mr Derek D. Johnston their Legal Services Adviser, for the part played by them in the process of compilation.

Many terms and expressions have been omitted because they seemed to the author not to be in common use (and for reasons of space). Can it really be said that "loco citato" is on everybody's lips. Indeed is it the case that the senior partner stalks round the corridors of office muttering "post hoc, ergo propter hoc" (in philosophical rather than in legal use). The latter has been included nonetheless as being a phrase which some with academic ambitions may tend to use.

It is hoped in particular that the publication will be of use to undergraduates, those taking law courses at technical colleges and others such as managers, trade union officials, businessmen and legal secretaries.

The point should perhaps be made that no compilation of relevant case law has been attempted in the publication and that no statutes passed after 1980 are taken into account.

It should perhaps also be mentioned that words in bold type in any part of the book are defined or explained elsewhere in it.

October 1981   J. A. BEATON

A

Ab initio.—This Latin tag has no specifically legal meaning. Its dictionary meaning is "from the beginning" and it is so used in legal matters.

Absolute discharge.—In certain circumstances the court which has found a person tried by them guilty of a crime or offence may, instead of sentencing the offender, make an order discharging him absolutely. This is competent where the offender is convicted on **indictment,** or where he is charged before a court of summary jurisdiction with an offence which the court is satisfied he committed. In either case the court must be of opinion, having regard to the circumstances, that it is inexpedient to inflict punishment and that a probation order is not appropriate. Where the case is before a **court of summary jurisdiction,** the court makes the order without convicting the offender. The granting of an absolute discharge is not competent where the penalty is fixed by statute.

Absolvitor.—A decree of *absolvitor* is one granted to the defender in a civil action. By pronouncing such a judgment the court absolves or decides finally in favour of the defender (see **Assoilzie**).

A caelo usque ad centrum.—The grant of a **feu** charter confers on the feur (vassal) the *dominium utile* (in effect ownership) not only of the whole ground described in the charter but also of all buildings, woods, waters, fishings and other property of any kind in or under the surface such as minerals or above it (the air space occupied for instance by the building). Thus what is owned is everything *a caelo usque ad centrum.* But there are many exceptions to this proposition. Planning law restricts the use to which land may be put, minerals are usually reserved to the superior and the use of air space by flying machines is provided for by legislation.

Access.—In the context of family law this relates to the access (*i.e.* opportunity to see, to visit, or to be, or live with) to which a parent (and in certain circumstances a grandparent) of a child under 16 who does not have custody of him or her is entitled, or is allowed by the court, to have. The court (in the case of an action of separation being the Court of Session or the sheriff court; in the case of an action of divorce or nullity the Court of Session) may deal with the question of custody. Where the question of custody arises out of any of the actions mentioned it is usually given to the parent who obtains decree in the action, although the mother has the stronger claim to custody of a child "of tender years" and there may of course be no dispute about custody. The parent not having, or who is refused, custody of a child, is normally entitled to reasonable opportunity to see the child or to have him or her stay with him or her perhaps during school holidays, by agreement or by order of the court. But the court may refuse access if the parent's circumstances, character or conduct render this undesirable in the child's interests.

Account of charge and discharge.—This is the form in which judicial factors, executors, trustees and others or their solicitors or other agents account, usually annually, for their dealings (usually referred to as intromissions) with the property in their care. The "charge" of the account first sets out the capital value of the property at the date at which the account begins and thereafter the income or other credits received out of the property. The "discharge" sets out first the payments made out of income and ends with a statement of the capital in hand at the close of the account. Any transactions with capital during the period of the account are also shown in the body of the account.

Accountant of Court.—The Accountant of Court is an officer of the Court of Session who supervises the conduct of **judicial factors** and others. He audits the factor's accounts annually and fixes the commission to which the factor is entitled. The accountant's audit and report are conclusive against a factor and he must report to the court any failure of duty on the part of the factor.

Accused.—Used as a verb, "accused" means that a person has been charged with the commission of a crime or offence. Used as a noun it means the person who has been so charged (see **Panel**).

Action.—This word is used in a general sense to refer to any civil proceedings which are brought before a court in which one party, the pursuer, seeks to obtain a remedy by way of a decree of court against the other party, the defender. An action is begun by the lodging in the court of a writ, usually called a "summons" if the action is in the Court of Session, or an "initial writ" if the action is in the sheriff court. Petitions are not usually referred to as actions and criminal proceedings never are. The pursuer must serve a copy of the initiating writ on the defender after the Clerk to the Signet has given written authority in a Court of Session action to the initiation (see **Citation**).

Acts of Adjournal.—Acts of Adjournal are made by the **High Court of Justiciary,** and contain rules for regulating procedure in criminal cases in that court, in the sheriff court when dealing with criminal cases, and in the district court. An Act of Adjournal is a statutory instrument. The Acts are published by. H.M. Stationery Office and are reproduced, *inter alia,* in the **Scots Law Times** and in the **Parliament House Book.**

Acts of Sederunt.—Acts of Sederunt are made by the **Court of Session** under powers conferred on it originally in the sixteenth century and by many statutes in recent times. Some Acts contain provisions of a legislative kind but most are concerned with the regulation of procedure followed in the Court of Session, in civil cases in the sheriff court and by administrative tribunals. They are statutory instruments and are published and reproduced in the same manner as Acts of Adjournal.

Adherence.—A husband and wife (spouses) should, the law provides, adhere to each other and cohabit at bed and board. The place of the matrimonial home is nowadays usually decided jointly but in strict law the husband still has the prior right to decide on its location and the duty to provide it. The wife has a duty to accompany him there provided it is reasonably suitable. If the house is the wife's the husband may, nowadays, be required to join the wife there. Refusal by either party to live in the house with the other would be desertion, justifying separation or divorce. If either spouse ceases to adhere without justification the other may seek to enforce the obligation by raising an action of adherence. The duty to adhere is not, however, specifically enforceable and the action to adhere is now, when used at all, always combined with an alternative crave for **aliment.**

Ad hoc.—A statement, proposition or decision made or applying only in relation to a particular case or in a specific set of circumstances is said to be made or to apply *ad hoc.*

Ad interim.—See **Aliment** for an example of a case in which this Latin expression is used. It could be translated as "in the meantime".

Adjudication.—In its broadest sense an adjudication is the process of determining a matter judicially. More narrowly it is the mode of attaching land in security, or in satisfaction, of sums owed by a debtor to a creditor, and is also the mode by which the creditor who is entitled to be **vested** in lands may obtain a title to them. Adjudication proceeds by way of action in the Court of Session. It is available only if there is a document by virtue of which the sums are actually payable (including a decree of court) and not contingent on some other event happening. If there is no such document there is a preliminary procedure of a complicated nature including, in certain circumstances, an action of **poinding of the ground.**

A decree of adjudication does not usually enable the creditor to dispose of the property adjudged. His right is a judicial security, not one of property, and the debtor may redeem the debt before the legal period of redemption, *i.e.* ten years. Thereafter the creditor must go through the process of **foreclosure.** If the debt is paid the adjudication is extinguished.

Adjudicator.—In the narrow sense this word is used in the context of the Immigration Act 1971. Any person arriving in the **United Kingdom** with a view to remaining in the country for a lengthy period is interviewed by Home (not Scottish) Office officials who decide whether he has a right, or may be permitted, to enter and remain in the country. The decision may be appealed to the Adjudicator whose appointment is made (after informal consultation with the Lord President) by the Home Secretary.

In a less specific sense the word has a meaning little different from that of the word "judge", but is not so used in Scots law.

Adjustment.—This is the name given to that part of the procedure in a civil action in court which enables a party to the action to alter written pleadings so as to introduce new material to meet the facts stated or allegations made by the other party or parties. Continuations of the case are granted by the court to enable adjustments to be finalised. The case is then ready to go to trial and (what is known as) the **record** is closed by the court. No further adjustment is possible without the leave of the court.

Ad longum.—A statement, proposition or document, set out at length or in full. The antithesis is a précis, epitome, abridgement, summary or synopsis.

Admissible evidence.—Evidence is the information made

available to a court by the parties to judicial proceedings. It is the means by which an unknown or disputed fact is made known (or proved) to the court. The information to be admissible must be both relevant to the proceedings and must conform to the laws of evidence. Evidence is, in general, relevant if it is logically connected with the matters in dispute between the parties. In more detail it is relevant if it is direct evidence of a fact bearing on the probability or improbability of a fact in issue (*i.e.* a matter in dispute), or evidence of a fact which has a bearing only on the admissibility of other evidence or on the credibility of a witness. The rules of the law of evidence are too numerous and complex to be dealt with here. But it must be remembered that not all evidence which is relevant is admissible. For example, a statement made by a person who is not a witness may be relevant but it may have to be disregarded if spoken to by some other person. It then becomes hearsay evidence which is (subject to some exceptions) inadmissible.

The same terms are used where the proceedings are before any other tribunal (*e.g.* an industrial, national insurance or supplementary benefit appeal tribunal) or an arbitration, but in those proceedings the strict rules of evidence may not apply. Whether these rules do or do not apply depends on the powers conferred (usually by statutory instrument) on the tribunal or in the case of an arbiter by the common law also.

Admonition.—If a person is guilty of a crime or offence the court will normally fine or imprison him. But if the offence is trifling or there are circumstances associated with the accused or the commission of the offence which satisfy the court that it would meet the justice of the cause, the guilty party will simply be dismissed by the court with an admonition. In practical terms this amounts perhaps to no more than a warning not to repeat the offence or to a mild reproof. The person is thus admonished.

Ad rem.—This expression is used to indicate that a decision, proposition or statement has a general significance and is not confined to a particular case or set of circumstances.

Ad valorem.—According to value. For instance, stamp duty on a deed may be fixed on an *ad valorem* basis — the value of the transaction to which the deed gives effect where no price or other quantum is specified.

Ad vitam aut culpam.—The duration of a contract of employment or of an appointment to an office or post is normally fixed by the terms of the contract itself or by the terms of the appointment. In the case of certain appointments however the duration is for life (*ad vitam*) or if and until some fault (*aut culpam*) *e.g.* misconduct, on the part of the incumbent is proved. There are few such appointments in modern times. Until recently all judicial appointments were held on this basis but judges of the Court of Session (except those appointed before 1959) are now required to retire at 75 years of age and sheriffs (since 1961) at 72 years. There is no age of retirement for honorary sheriffs (see also **Justice of the Peace**).

Advocate.—In general terms this means as a noun a person who pleads the cause (the case) of another and, as a verb, it means to plead a cause.

In a more restricted sense it refers to a member of the Faculty of Advocates, which is the governing body of the Scottish Bar. Advocates have the exclusive right to appear in cases before the High Court of Justiciary and the Court of Session and may also plead in Scottish civil cases in the House of Lords and any other court or administrative tribunal in Scotland. Advocates also give opinions on difficult legal problems referred to them by solicitors on behalf of clients. After a number of years in practice an advocate (called "junior counsel") may be appointed a Q.C. (Queen's Counsel) by the Queen on the recommendation of the **Lord President.** This is called "taking silk" because "senior counsel" as he then has become, must wear a gown of silk (see **Counsel**). An advocate may be instructed only through an admitted solicitor, and if a client has a consultation with his counsel the solicitor will be present.

The word advocate is also used to refer to a solicitor who is a member of the Society of Advocates in Aberdeen.

Advocate Depute.—An advocate depute is an advocate appointed by the Lord Advocate to assist him and the Solicitor-General in the discharge of their functions — mainly those in the criminal field. There are currently seven advocates depute. They (as well as technically the Lord Advocate and Solicitor-General) are known as Crown counsel. Each is assigned to one of the four circuits into which Scotland is divided for the purpose of criminal administration, and he deals with cases reported to the Crown Office from that circuit by **procurators fiscal.** In addition to dealing with criminal matters in the Crown Office he may also prosecute cases which come before the High Court of Justiciary and in all but the most serious criminal cases which come before the circuit courts.

Affidavit.—This is a written statement signed by a person who has been put on oath by an official (*e.g.* a **notary public**) who has authority to administer the oath. It is not commonly in use in Scotland as a means of furnishing proof of a fact, but is extensively used in England. It is coming into more frequent use in Scotland, however, and a recent addition to the circumstances in which it can be used in Scotland is to be found in divorce law. The Act of Sederunt (Rules of Court Amendment No. 1) (Consistorial Causes) 1978 provides that in undefended actions for divorce and separation and aliment the necessary evidence may be given by affidavit.

Affiliation.—This word is most frequently used in a legal context in relation to illegitimate children. Where the paternity of a child is doubtful or disputed, an **action** may be brought by the child's mother or, if the mother is dead, by the child's **tutor,** to have it determined whether the person against whom the action is brought is the father. The action is usually combined with one for **aliment** and, if the court grants decree of affiliation against the alleged father, an order against him for payment of aliment will follow automatically. The word affiliation itself is a noun derived from the verb "affiliate" which means "to impute paternity".

It also has the meaning of associating or being closely connected with, as a branch of a larger organisation, and in this sense is perhaps most well known in the context of the law about trade union and labour relations. Most unions are affiliated to the Trades Union Congress and some are affiliated to the Labour Party. In neither case does this mean that they belong to the Congress or the Party; they merely become associated or closely connected with the one or the other.

A fortiori.—This Latin phrase is used of facts, things, statements or anything which provides support for the correctness of some proposition or argument or which, because the proposition is admitted to be correct, must, it follows, also be correct. Literal translations could be "by a stronger argument" or "so much the more".

Agent.—An agent is a person who undertakes to carry out work or execute business for reward (in the absence of reward the function is one of **mandate**) on behalf of another termed the "principal". The principal and the agent enter into a contract by which the former authorises the latter to carry out the work or execute the business. Whether a person is an agent or not may be difficult to establish. The authority is not necessarily given in writing or even expressly. It may be implied or inferred from the actings of the parties or it may be constituted by ratification of actings of an ostensible agent. Whether the relationship is one of agency or not is a question of fact (see **Law agent**).

Alias.—Literally this word means "otherwise". More specifically and used more frequently in a legal context, it means a name assumed usually with criminal intent.

Alien.—Any person resident or working in any part of the United Kingdom who is not a British subject is an alien. Not all citizens of the UK are British subjects. Citizens of Commonwealth countries give rise to difficulties and UK membership of the European Economic Community has altered the situation. The British Nationality Acts 1948 to 1965 and the Immigration Act 1971 are the main statutes dealing with the matter. The Home Secretary keeps a central register of all aliens and every chief constable keeps a register of aliens resident or working within the police area. Aliens are required to register with the police when they enter the UK and to re-register when they move from one part of the country to another.

Aliment.—In its broadest sense aliment means nourishment, food and provision for maintenance. It has several more specific meanings in law:

(1) Its narrowest meaning is the amount of money which a court has found that one person has a duty, and is financially able, to pay to another for the other's maintenance, the other being without means of supplying himself or herself with food, clothing, lodging and other necessaries of livelihood.

(2) Less narrowly it refers to the duty which a person has to contribute to the maintenance of certain of his or her relatives if the former is financially able to do so and the latter are in need. For instance a husband and father has a duty to aliment (maintain) his wife and children.

The husband normally discharges his duty to his wife by providing a home and funds to maintain her if she is unable to maintain herself.

The father's duty to maintain his child lasts, in all circumstances, so long as the child is under the age of puberty; 12 years if a girl, or 14 if a boy. Now that the school leaving age is 16 the duty probably exists in both cases until that age is attained. From puberty onwards the duty is to maintain the child until he or she can legally and in fact maintain himself or herself by his or her own exertions. The duty may also be for life if the child is by reason of physical or mental incapacity, or inability to obtain employment, unable to support himself or herself.

A wife and mother has similar duties to aliment her husband and children. Where both father and mother are alive the father has the primary duty to maintain the children, even if the mother is employed and has a greater superfluity of means than he has.

The parents of an illegitimate child also have a duty to maintain the child. Special rules apply.

(3) There are a number of other circumstances in which the law imposes a duty on one party to aliment another. For instance if the father and mother of a child are dead the child may seek to be alimented firstly by his own children, if he has any, and then, if he is legitimate, by his grandfathers and grandmothers or more remote ascendants but only in a certain order. These duties are infrequently relied on.

(4) Children, other than illegitimate children, have a reciprocal duty to aliment their indigent parents. As a father is not obliged to aliment his daughter-in-law or son-in-law there is no reciprocal claim available to the parents-in-law.

(5) Where the parties have been divorced or judicially separated, the party who is awarded custody of the children of the marriage may be granted an award of aliment for the children. But payment of a lump sum or a periodical payment ordered by the court to be made by the divorced spouse to the divorcing spouse is not a payment of aliment.

(6) The aliment to be made available is, in the absence of agreement, fixed by the court and its amount depends on the social and financial position of the parents and on the parent in question having means superfluous to those he or she requires to maintain himself or herself. A spouse's position is similar.

Allenarly.—In ordinary usage this word means "only" or "solely". In law it is used to make clear that the bequest of property to which the word is applied is made in **liferent** only and is not to be construed as conferring the **fee** of the property on the beneficiary.

Allodial land.—Allodial land is land owned outright and absolutely. It is an exceptional mode of ownership, most land being held on feudal tenure. Land held by the Crown, land used for churches, churchyards, manses and glebes is allodial. So also is some land in Orkney and Shetland which is **udal land.** Land acquired compulsorily under statute is in a similar position (see also **Disposition**).

Amnesty.—Amnesty is a pardon granted by the Crown or by the governing body of a country to all, or to a particular class of, persons who have been kept in custody. They will have been so dealt with for the commission of what are regarded as crimes of any category or crimes of a particular class or the taking of actions or actions of a particular class not necessarily crimes, usually having political objectives. In Great Britain as a whole, this is of little importance but in Northern Ireland the position is different. An amnesty granted in a foreign country may affect citizens in Great Britain.

Appellant.—A person who appeals to a higher court against the decision of a lower court is called an appellant. The Inner House of the Court of Session has jurisdiction in appeals against the decision of a Lord Ordinary and of a sheriff principal or a sheriff in a civil case. The sheriff principal has jurisdiction to hear appeals in such cases from the decision of any sheriff in his sheriffdom. Most, though not all, Court of Session decisions may be appealed to the House of Lords. In criminal cases decided in the sheriff or district courts the appeals are to the High Court of Justiciary.

Not all decisions can be appealed against. In some matters certain courts have sole or, as it is called, privative jurisdiction. For instance, decisions of the Lands Valuation Appeal Court cannot be appealed against. In many cases any appeal available is on a question of law but not on a question of fact. This is particularly true of appeals by way of a **stated case** in which the facts are stated by the lower court or tribunal and cannot be re-tried.

Apportionment.—This word in general usage means the division or adjustment of any thing, right, or property into just or due shares. At common law the ownership of many kinds of periodical payments, *e.g.* rents, did not emerge until the date of payment, whereas interest on money and profits of daily work, including wages, became from day to day the property of the person entitled to them. The Apportionment Act 1870, however, provides that unless it is stipulated that no apportionment is to be made, all annuities, rents, dividends and other periodical payments in the nature of income are to be treated as accruing from day to day and are apportionable accordingly both as respects the duty to pay and the right to receive the payments.

A priori.—This word has no specific legal meaning. It is used more in a philosophical context, being applied to reasoning from what is prior, logically or chronologically, *e.g.* reasoning from cause to effect. **A posteriori** is the antithesis.

Arbiter.—See **Arbitration.**

Arbitration.—Arbitration is the adjudication of a dispute or controversy, over fact or law or both, outside the ordinary civil courts by one or more persons to whom the parties who are in dispute refer the matter for decision. The reference of certain kinds of dispute to arbitration is required by statute or is provided for in a contract between parties often as an alternative and in preference to going to court. An arbiter's decision is always final on fact but an appeal on a question of law may be available to the Court of Session. It is competent for a judge of the Court of Session to accept appointment as an arbiter.

Arrestment.—Arrestment (a form of **Diligence**) is the process by which a creditor ensures that the money and moveable effects of his debtor which are in the hands of a third party are not made over to the debtor. The money which may be arrested includes wages due but unpaid and arrestment of wages is the use to which this is most frequently put. Where wages are paid weekly or monthly the wages payable in respect of that part of the week or month already gone when the arrestment is effected are detained in the hands of the employer. Arrestment has the effect of attaching the property arrested (but not of course in the debtor's own possession.) An arrestment in these circumstances is used by a creditor (known as the "arrestor") holding a decree of court (it can be used in other circumstances also), an extract of which is sufficient warrant for the purpose. A schedule is served on (*i.e.* sent to) the person (known as the "arrestee") in whose possession the moveables are or who is to pay the wages. This is known as "arrestment in execution".

Another form is "arrestment on the dependence" of an action and is used when an action for payment of money has been or is about to be initiated by the creditor. It is a means of obtaining security for the debt. If the creditor obtains a decree in the action he has a preferable right over the property arrested, which then becomes equivalent to an arrestment in execution.

Yet another form is arrestment to found jurisdiction. In this case a person in Scotland who wishes to raise a personal action in a Scottish court against somebody over whom the Scottish courts would not otherwise have jurisdiction can arrest moveable property in Scotland which belongs to the foreigner. The rules of jurisdiction of the EEC refuse to countenance this as a ground of jurisdiction, but this does not affect its use in relation to persons domiciled in the other countries of the UK.

Two points to be noted are that the legal costs of effecting the arrestment of wages are paid by the debtor and that an arrangement is therefore frequently made between creditor, debtor and employer for a certain sum of wages payable in any week (or month) to be paid by the employer direct to the creditor. (See also **Furthcoming**.)

Articles of roup.—Where land is sold by public auction, the conditions of the contract into which the purchaser enters with the seller are usually contained in a document called articles of roup. Appended to the document is another in which are set out the preference as purchaser of the highest offerer and the purchase price. The latter document must be signed by or on behalf of both purchaser and seller. (See **Public Roup**.)

Art and Part.—This is an expression used in the context of criminal law and means broadly, acting in the capacity of an accessory or accomplice. Its origin is uncertain. It may mean either by contrivance (art) or actual participation (part) or it may be that "art" at one time applied to the actor. In any event every criminal charge now implicitly contains the words "actor or art and part" so that if the charge relates to the theft of a watch or an assault, the person charged can be convicted, whether it is proved that he actually took the watch or committed the assault or only that he was an accessory to the theft or the assault.

Assessor.—In its most common usage this term means the person employed by a local authority (the "regional assessor") to assess the value (gross and net annual and rateable values) to be placed on all property within the authority's area on which the authority are empowered to levy rates. He does not levy or collect rates. A second meaning of the word is a person who assists a judge who is hearing an action by providing information and views on special features of the evidence with which he (the assessor) is specially familiar and of which the judge must be in possession to enable him to decide the action.

Assignation.—A right to **incorporeal moveable property** can be transferred by assignation granted by the owner (also the "cedent" or "assignor") to the assignee. Some rights, such as those which are alimentary, are not assignable and some may be in security only. The document of transfer is called an Assignation and, though no particular words of transfer are required, care must be taken to make clear what property is being transferred and whether the transfer is outright or in security. The term applies also to the transfer of other rights *e.g.* rights under a lease.

Assoilzie.—To free or decide finally in favour of a defender of a claim or charge.

Attestation.—Attestation is the subscription by a person of his name to a deed, will or other document and, in some instances, by witnesses for the purpose of authenticating or testifying to the genuineness of the subscription. The formal authentication of deeds is regulated by statutes which prescribe the solemnities to be complied with. For this purpose writs can be placed broadly in three categories — those which are solemnly attested deeds (*e.g.* deeds transferring the ownership of heritable property); holograph writings which require to be written and subscribed by the granter with his name; writings in *re mercatoria* and writings which enjoy statutory privilege. (See **Notarial execution; Obligationes Literis; Re mercatoria; Privilege; Holograph.**)

Attorney.—See **Power of Attorney.**

Auction.—An auction is a public sale at which goods are offered for sale in lots each lot being sold to the person who makes the highest bid for it.

Audi alteram partem.—This expression, virtually the antithesis of *ex parte,* signifies that both parties in any proceedings before a court or other tribunal should be heard before a decision is reached.

Auditor of Court.—The Auditor of the Court of Session is appointed by the Secretary of State. The Court of Session may remit to him the accounts of parties (fees and outlays of counsel and solicitor) to civil actions which have come before them. These are referred to as judicial audits. He may also audit the accounts and fees charged by solicitors in dealing with trust or executry estates or other non-judicial audits. For example, a client can ask the auditor to fix a fee if he is unhappy about the expenses but this involves paying both the solicitor and the auditor. The auditor is paid a salary for the performance of judicial audits and retains fees paid to him for carrying out private audits. He has a staff to assist him, the members of which are appointed by himself and are paid such salaries out of his own funds as he himself negotiates. (See also **Taxation of Accounts.**)

In the sheriff court, the **sheriff clerk** may perform similar functions, or a solicitor may be appointed by the sheriff to do so.

Averment.—This means simply a statement positively made, something declared to be true. (See **Pleading.**)

Avizandum.—This Latin tag is much used in the context of court proceedings. The judge or judges of any court before whom proceedings (except summary proceedings) have taken place may give judgment immediately on the termination of the proceedings or they may take time to consider the case, reach their decisions and write their judgments. In the latter instance the court is said "to make avizandum" or "take the case to avizandum". The phrase is used colloquially by others in non-legal spheres as meaning the taking of time to decide what they should do next.

B

Back letter—See **ex facie absolute disposition.**

Bail.—All crimes and offences (whether common law or statutory) are bailable except murder and treason. Simply put, this means that when a person is charged with a crime other than murder or treason or an offence, he is entitled, immediately after he has been brought before the sheriff or district court, to apply to the court for liberation on bail. The prosecutor is entitled to be heard on every such application and the sheriff or district court is entitled in its discretion to refuse the application if the circumstances in their view make it unwise that the accused should be at large. A right of appeal against a refusal is available only after committal for trial or further examination.

The Bail etc, (Scotland) Act 1980 altered the law substantially so far as it relates to the conditions on which a person could be released on bail. Before it came into operation on 1 April 1980 bail was obtainable only by a deposit of money with the court (or in minor instances with the police) or the finding of caution for the amount of the bail money fixed. The 1980 Act made it unlawful "to grant bail or release for a pledge or deposit of money" and in place thereof provided that release on bail may be granted only on conditions which are not to include a pledge or deposit but preserves the provisions about the granting of liberation by the police set out in ss. 18, 294, 295 and 296 of the Criminal Justice (Scotland) Act 1975 as amended by ss. 7 and 8 of the 1980 Act.

The conditions on which bail may now be granted are set out in the 1980 Act, but provision is made for the imposition of additional conditions. An instance of such an additional condition is that the accused's passport should be deposited in court.

Bankruptcy.—Bankruptcy is a general term used to describe the state of or stage in a person's affairs (usually business affairs) when he is unable to meet his financial commitments. **Sequestration** which may follow on bankruptcy is dealt with elsewhere in this glossary. It is the name given to the stage when the bankrupt person's property is taken out of his hands and put under official control. There is an earlier stage at which a person is said to be bankrupt. This is when he is insolvent and is unable or refuses to meet current obligations even if his total assets would enable him to do so. There is another stage, namely the

11

stage at which a person's bankruptcy has become publicly known. He is then said to be *notour bankrupt* and this stage is reached if he is facing sequestration or when his insolvency has become manifest by, for instance, his failure to repay on the date fixed for repayment sums borrowed by him. Jurisdiction in cases of bankruptcy is dealt with in ss. 11 and 16 of the Bankruptcy (Scotland) Act 1913 as amended by the Law Reform (Miscellaneous Provisions) (Scotland) Act 1980.

Blood test.—This phrase derives from wording first used in the Road Safety Act 1967 and now appearing in ss. 6-10 of the Road Traffic Act 1972. The 1972 Act makes provision enabling a constable to require a person who has been arrested under ss. 5 or 8 of the Act, to provide at a police station a specimen of his blood or urine which is then subjected to a laboratory test designed to establish whether or not the proportion of alcohol in his blood exceeds the prescribed limit of 80 mg. of alcohol in 100 ml. of blood.

Bona fides.—Good faith; without fraud or deceit.

Bond.—A written obligation to pay money or to do some act, *e.g.* under a bond of caution one person undertakes to act as surety for another in the other's performance of some function he has undertaken.

Bond and disposition in security.—Until the introduction of the **standard security** in 1970, a very common procedure followed by a lender of money who wished to obtain security for repayment was to require the borrower to grant a bond imposing on the latter an obligation to repay with interest the sum borrowed and a disposition of heritage owned by the latter which the lender was empowered to sell in the event of the obligation to repay not being complied with.

Books of Council and Session.—Until the early nineteenth century it was competent by virtue of long-standing custom to register deeds for preservation or execution in the books of the Lords of Council and Session, in the books of the sheriff courts and in certain other books. The Public Records (Scotland) Act 1809 restricted registration to the Books of Council and Session and sheriff court books. The former are kept by the Keeper of the Registers and a very wide variety of deeds are registered in them. The sheriff court books are less used now.

Breach of contract.—Breach of contract consists in the failure by a contracting party to implement any of the terms of the contract incumbent on that party. The party who alleges that the other is in breach must prove in what respects the other has failed to perform his part properly, and if he succeeds in the proof, he is entitled to damages in an action raised by him for the purpose. Breach may also entitle the injured party in some circumstances to refuse to perform the obligations incumbent on him or to rescind the contract and claim damages on the basis of a total failure to perform.

Breach of the peace.—In ordinary language this phrase means a lesser form of mobbing and rioting. Typically, a breach of the peace is a public disturbance such as brawling or fighting in public, shouting and swearing in the street or any general tumult or conduct interfering with the peace of the neighbourhood.

Whether or not any particular acts amount to such a disturbance is a question of fact. In practice no distinction is made at common law between breach of the peace and conduct which is simply disorderly. The foregoing are excerpts from Sheriff G. H. Gordon's *Criminal Law.*

In addition to being a lesser form of riot the offence of breach of the peace is used as a way of maintaining order, decency and of enabling the police to carry out their task of preserving public order. Any conduct which appears calculated to provoke an actual disturbance of the peace is thus itself regarded as constituting an offence. This has considerable practical importance and has been much developed in recent years so that actings which are themselves far removed from the creation of public disturbance are now treated as offences. Conduct likely to cause alarm or annoyance which could lead to actual disturbance is also an offence and so also are threats likely to place the threatened person in a state of fear and alarm.

Breath test.—This phrase derives from the wording of the Road Traffic Act 1972 which provides for tests of a person's breath for the purpose of obtaining an indication of the proportion of alcohol in his blood. The tests are carried out by means of a device of a type approved for the purpose by the Secretary of State. Any person driving or attempting to drive a motor vehicle on a road or other public place has a duty to provide a specimen of his breath when required to do so by a constable in uniform who has reasonable cause for suspecting him of having alcohol in his body or having committed a traffic offence while the vehicle was in motion. One breath test is made at the roadside as a rule and, if positive, the person may be arrested and must be given an opportunity to provide a specimen at the police station. This provision also applies where an accident has occurred. In such a case a driver of a vehicle involved in an accident can be required by a constable in uniform to give a specimen of breath either where the requirement is made or at a police station or, where the driver is in hospital as a patient, at the hospital.

Burden.—In its ordinary sense this word (which is well known) means a load, weight or cargo. Its special legal meaning is any restriction, limitation or encumbrance affecting a person or property. Thus the obligation which one person, a husband perhaps, has to maintain another (the wife or child) is a burden which he is obliged to bear.

More usually, however, the expression is used in relation to land or other heritable property. If the owner of the house borrows money, granting over the house a **standard security,** he is personally and the land is said to be, burdened with an obligation to repay. Feudal conditions (*e.g.* restrictions or limitations on the use to which land may be put, servitudes such as a private right of way, or obligations to make a periodical payment in respect of land, *e.g.* a feuduty) are all burdens on the land and its owner.

Burden of proof.—In a civil action before any court the onus of proving the case or any particular fact or point of law which arises in it, rests upon the party who is putting it forward as being correct. In most cases the onus is on the pursuer, *e.g.* a person who is claiming damages for injuries received in a road traffic accident or who is seeking to divorce his or her spouse or who is asking the court to interdict somebody else from doing something or taking some action which the pursuer believes to be unlawful. But if the defender in any action pleads that the facts are different from those alleged by the pursuer it is for him, the defender, to prove his version of them if the pursuer's evidence is sufficient to prove his own allegations. The standard of proof as a general rule is that the inference which is more probable will prevail. The decision is said to turn upon a "balance of probabilities". If an action is not defended then, except in a case where the law requires the pursuer's case to be proved (*e.g.* an action of divorce or of separation and custody), no proof is called for.

In criminal cases the prosecution has to prove guilt beyond reasonable doubt (*i.e.* the burden of proof is on them). The statement "a person is innocent until he is proved guilty" accurately expresses the law.

By-law (also **bye-law**).—The word by-law is most frequently used to describe rules or regulations made by a local authority. They are a form of **subordinate legislation** and have a status and effect not very dissimilar from other forms of subordinate legislation. Every local authority (*i.e.* regional and district councils) is given powers by statute to make by-laws (see ss. 201-204 of the Local Government (Scotland) Act 1973) for the good rule and government of the whole or any part of the area of the authority's responsibility. By-laws normally have to be confirmed by a higher authority such as the Secretary of State or the sheriff, and are open to challenge as being **ultra vires** or unreasonable or contrary to the general law. As in the case of other subordinate legislation, a by-law is impliedly revoked if the authorising statute is repealed.

By-laws may also be made by boards, corporations (both public and private) and companies under statutory powers for the government of their proceedings and management of their business.

C

Candlemas.—Candlemas, the second day of February (the festival of the purification of the Virgin Mary), is a quarter day in Scotland having similar importance legally as Lammas. (See **Lammas**.)

Case or **cause**.—These words are simply alternatives by which an action or other proceedings in a civil court are referred to.

Case law.—This is law embodied in decisions of the courts. The decisions given by a superior court, *e.g.* the Court of Session, must be followed in any later similar case by an inferior court, *e.g.* the sheriff court, but there may be argument as to whether the facts of the case decided by the superior court are the same as those in the case before the inferior court and thus whether the decision in the former must be followed.

Reported Scottish decisions may be found in the volumes of

Session Cases which have been published annually for two centuries and periodically before then. They also appear in the *Scots Law Times*. Reports of sheriff court cases appear in the *Scots Law Times* and in earlier legal journals such as the *Scottish Law Review*. Cases decided by administrative tribunals and the Land Court are separately reported, as are decisions of the EEC Court of Justice.

Causa.—Most frequently used in the context of court proceedings (a cause) but in a more general sense means any issue which gives rise to contention.

Causa causans.—This refers to the real dominant or effective cause of the harm caused by a breach of a duty; the immediate cause, the *causa proxima,* the last link in the chain of causation.

Causa sine qua non.—This expression is used in the context of the law of obligations to mean an essential cause. But it may also mean a casual factor of harm done which is a prerequisite or essential factor leading to the harm done.

Cause.—See **Case.**

Caution.—In certain fields of law a person who is carrying out some function is required to obtain security (caution) to ensure that he carries out his task properly. For instance an **executor dative** has to obtain caution to guard against maladministration, as, perhaps, by making away with the executry funds. Insurance companies are normally relied on to provide this form of security by means of a bond of caution for which a single premium is paid.

Certification Officer.—This is a name first given by the Industrial Relations Act 1971 (now to be found in the Employment Protection Act 1975) to an officer of the Advisory, Conciliation and Arbitration Service set up under s. 1 of the Employment Protection Act 1975. The following is, briefly, his position. The 1975 Act transferred to the Certification Officer from the Registrar of Friendly Societies the functions the latter performed in relation to trade unions under the Trade Union Act 1913, the Trade Union (Amalgamation) Act 1964 and the Trade Union and Labour Relations Act 1974. The 1974 Act provided that one function of the registrar is to maintain separate lists of trade unions and employers' associations either registered before the Industrial Relations Act 1971 came into operation or under it.

An extensive list of requirements set out in the 1971 Act if satisfied by a trade union enabled it to obtain a certificate that it was an independent trade union. The officer was given power to issue or refuse a certificate without stating reasons for doing so. He could also withdraw a certificate after notification to the union of his intention to do so, if in his opinion, it had ceased to be independent. The certificate is conclusive evidence of the independence of the union. A certificate cannot be issued to a trade union which is not on the list. Thus to obtain a certificate a union must first obtain admission to the list. An appeal against a decision of the officer to grant or refuse or withdraw a certificate may be made to the Employment Appeal Tribunal.

Charge.—The word "charge" means generally an order to obey a decree of court but it has two distinct meanings in Scots law. It is firstly important in the case of a defender (debtor) against whom the court has granted a decree. In this context it means a procedural step which must be taken by the pursuer (creditor) before he can enforce the decree by seizure and sale of the debtor's goods — a process known as **poinding.** Thus, if the decree requires payment of a sum of money, there must be served on the debtor by a **sheriff officer** a document in a specified form requesting the debtor to pay the sum due and warning him that if he does not pay within the number of days stated (the days of charge are of varying number according to the statutory provision involved) his goods will be poinded. (See **Warrant Sale.**)

"Charge" is also the word used to signify the means laid down by statute (the Companies (Floating Charges and Receivers) (Scotland) Act 1972) by which a security for borrowed money is created over property belonging to a company.

Chartulary.—A volume in which copies of feus, leases and other deeds relating to landed estate are gathered together (formerly engrossed) for private record purposes.

Children's hearing.—Children's hearings are part of the structure provided by the Social Work (Scotland) Act 1968 for dealing with children "in need of compulsory measures of care". Part III of that Act contains all the provisions relevant to hearings, and s. 34 of that part is the foundation for them. That section enacts that each hearing is to be held by a tribunal consisting of three members of the children's panel set up under s. 33 of and Schedule 3 to the Act; the three are a chairman and two others, one of each sex. Section 35 contains detailed provisions about the time, place, privacy and notification of a hearing and provides that rules for the constitution and arranging of, and procedure at, hearings are to be made by the Secretary of State. The rules in force at the time of writing are the Children's Hearings (Scotland) Rules 1971. Hearings are held in a number of circumstances. Section 37 (4) of the Act requires that a children's hearing is to be arranged where the **reporter** considers that a child may be in need of compulsory measures of care and the remaining provisions of that section and those of the ensuing sections contain further detailed provisions of the steps to be taken before, during and after the hearing and of the decisions to which the tribunal may come.

Citation.—When a person wishes to begin civil proceedings against another a summons (and other papers) is lodged by him in court and the solicitor conducting the case or a sheriff officer serves a citation on the person who will become the defender. The citation gives notice of the raising of an action and requires the defender to appear in court on a specified day if he proposes to defend.

Similarly in criminal proceedings the prosecutor (in a case where the accused person is not in the custody of the police) serves a citation on the accused person telling him on what day he has to answer to the charge against him either by attendance in court or, where permitted, by letter.

The word is also used in its verbal form, *e.g.* a witness in a case is cited to be at court on the day on which the case in which he is required to give evidence is to be before the court.

Citation and cite also have a further meaning. An advocate or solicitor may cite a case as being a *precedent* in his favour; the citation may be simply the name of the case (*e.g.* X *v.* Y), or may consist of the reading of passages from the judgment in the case.

Cite.—See **Citation.**

Civil action.—An action raised in a court which deals with a matter of **civil law,** is referred to as a civil action.

Civil law.—Civil law is the law which applies for the regulation of rights and duties and settlement of disputes between Natural or **Legal Persons.** The expression "civil action" means a case which is brought before the court for decision about any right or duty. The decision confers on the party in whose favour it is granted the right to enforce it.

Closed record.—See **Record.**

Codicil.—A codicil is a testamentary writing which adds to, revokes part of, or otherwise modifies, a **will** made earlier. There may be any number of codicils to a will. The will and all codicils to it must be looked at together and interpreted and construed as one testamentary document. Signed alterations to a copy of a will, and testamentary documents in the testator's handwriting are accepted as codicils. Even an unsigned list in the testator's handwriting of the names of intended beneficiaries has, in the special circumstances of the case, been accepted as forming part of a codicil.

Collateral.—In family law a collateral relative means, in relation to any person, any other person who is descended from the same ancestor but not in the direct line. Thus brothers and sisters are collateral relatives to each other but, for instance, fathers and sons, grandfathers and grandsons, whose relationship to each other is regarded as being in the direct line, are not. The question of collateral relationship is of importance in the field of **Aliment.** A person enriched by the succession to his parents' estate may be bound, as representing his parents, to aliment his brothers and sisters.

The word collateral is used also in other fields of law. In succession it has the same meaning as in family law, but a collateral security for instance, is security auxiliary to the principal security granted to the lender of money so as the better to secure payment of sums of interest on, and repayment of, the money lent.

Collation.—This word is used in the context of the law of succession, in which it has a meaning similar to its general meaning — a bringing together for comparison and examination. Before 1964 it applied to two aspects of the law; there is now only one. Collation between heirs (*inter haeredes*) ceased to have any significance with the passing of the Succession (Scotland) Act 1964 under which intestate succession to **heritage** became the same as intestate succession to **moveables.** The field in which collation still exists is collation between children (*inter liberos*). Its effect is that any child who has during the deceased's parent's lifetime received advances must in general collate the advances, which are then added to the **legitim** fund and thereafter set off against the share to which that child is entitled on equal division of the whole fund amongst all the children.

Commissary.—The commissary was originally an ecclesiastical judge who dealt with cases relating to such matters as legitimacy, succession and declarator of marriage. The word is now used almost wholly in relation to that part of the sheriff court which deals with such commissary matters connected with succession (*e.g.* appointment of **executors dative**) as are now within its jurisdiction. There is one statutory function of the sheriff clerk which should be noted in this connection. Where the estate in an executry has a value of less than £10,000, application may be made by the executor to the sheriff clerk who then completes an inventory, has it testified to by the applicant on oath and recorded. The sheriff clerk then issues confirmation to the executor.

Commissioner for Local Administration in Scotland.—The Commissioner for Local Administration in Scotland conducts investigations into acts and actions of certain authorities and he may make recommendations to the authorities or to government departments or may state the conclusions he has reached as the result of any investigation. Section 23 of the Local Government (Scotland) Act 1975 should be consulted.

The commissioner does not undertake the investigation of a complaint *ex proprio motu.* The complaint must be made by a regional or district councillor by or on behalf of a member of the public who claims to have suffered injustice in consequence of maladministration by a local authority and may be investigated by the commissioner after it has been brought to the notice of the authority. Sections 24-27 of the 1975 Act contain provisions about the manner in which and time within which a complaint may be made, the persons who may make a complaint, about circumstances in which no investigation may be undertaken, about the authority's right to comment, the commissioner's right to obtain information and documents, payment of expenses, disclosure of information so obtained and obstruction of the commissioner, all of which are similar to those which appear in the 1967 Act in relation to the **Parliamentary Commissioner for Administration.**

Section 28 of the 1975 Act requires that the commissioner will submit a report of any investigation to the person who referred it to him, and to the complainer and the authority concerned. Section 29 deals with cases in which the commissioner is satisfied that injustice has been caused and there are also provisions modifying the law of defamation in relation to, and limiting the disclosure of information by, the commissioner, Provision is also made for consultation between the commissioner, the Parliamentary Commissioner for Administration and the **Health Service Commissioner** about any complaint which relates partly to a matter within the sphere of one or both of the others.

Committal.—A person who has been charged with a serious crime may be committed to remain in an institution pending his trial on **indictment.** Special rules apply in the cases of persons under 21 years of age (see ss. 23-25 of the Criminal Procedure (Scotland) Act 1975).

Common debtor.—When a person ("A") owes money to

another ("B") and "B" obtains payment of the money by arresting (see **Arrestment**) money belonging or payable to "A" by a third party ("X") in whose hands it is, "A" is known as the "common debtor".

Common law.—Broadly speaking, common law in Scotland means any law which does not have statute as its source. It includes law made by judges (see **Case law**) and the law which is to be found in legal books and treatises having "Institutional" authority. Examples of the second category are the *Institutions of the Law of Scotland* written by Lord Stair (Sir James Dalrymple) when he was Lord President of the Court of Session and published in 1681. It has been said that Lord Stair set out the whole of Scots law as a rational, comprehensive, coherent and practical system of rules deduced from common sense principles. Other institutional writers followed him. Erskine published his *Institute* in 1773 and Bell his *Commentaries* in 1800. Baron Hume's *Commentaries* (early nineteenth century) set out systematically Scottish criminal law. It is difficult to say to what extent the early Celtic law of Scotland and custom have left their mark on Scots law, but some aspects of the pre-Reformation canon law are still to be seen, particularly in the law relating to wills and to winding-up of estates. (See **Commissary.**)

Community service order.—The Community Service by Offenders (Scotland) Act 1979 provided for a person convicted of a crime or offence to carry out work useful to the community instead of being penalised by fine or imprisonment. It came into force on 1 February 1979 but is as yet actually in operation only in a small number of areas in Scotland. The scope of its application is however being gradually increased. (It does not, of course, apply to England, where however a similar Act has been enacted.)

Compensation by offenders.—Part IV of the Criminal Justice (Scotland) Act 1980 makes provision — for the first time in statute — for the payment of compensation by a person convicted of an offence which has caused injury, loss or damage to another. The compensation is payable to the injured party.

Complaint.—A complaint is the form in which a criminal charge is made in summary proceedings in the sheriff court. The charge is made at the instance of the procurator fiscal or in private prosecutions (which are almost unknown) by the person who is raising the proceedings.

Composition contract.—A composition contract may be entered into by the creditors of a person who is unable to meet his debts in full. This is not regulated by statute, and is thus known as being extra-judicial. It is not to be confused with a composition accepted by creditors. If creditors are willing to let their debtor continue in business as if he were solvent, they may agree to accept a composition (a compromise) of their debts in full discharge of the debtor's obligations. It is implied in the contract that all will be treated equally and that the debtor has made a full disclosure of his estate and the extent of his insolvency. The concurrence of all creditors must be obtained and provision is made for security for payment and for the debtor's discharge.

Compos mentis.—"Of sound mind"; "sane".

Conclusion.—In a **Summons** a statement of the claim or claims (also referred to as the "precise relief") for which decree by the court is sought, appears at the end of the formal portion of the summons. This is known as the conclusion or, if there is more than one (as there usually is), the conclusions of the summons, and it states the precise relief sought.

Condescendence.—This is the name given to the part of the written pleadings of the pursuer in a court action, whether in a **summons** or **initial writ,** which contains a statement of the facts on which he relies and which, if he is to succeed, he will be obliged to prove in so far as they are not admitted by the defender.

Conditio si institutus sine liberis decesserit.—This expresses a principle of the Scots law of succession which has a purpose similar to that of the **conditio si testator sine liberis decesserit.** It applies where there has been a bequest made by will to descendants of the testator or to his nephews or nieces and their descendants. If any such beneficiary should die before the testator, then his **issue** may take the share of the estate to which he would have been entitled had he survived the testator.

Conditio si testator sine liberis decesserit.—This Latin phrase expresses a principle of the Scots law of **succession.** A rough rendering of its meaning is: the remedy which the law makes available to a child or children born to a parent who, having made a **will** which makes no provision for the child or children, dies without altering the will or making a new one to take account of the existence of the child or children. In such circumstances the law presumes that the will has been revoked, on the view that had the child or children been alive when the will was made it would have contained provisions in his, her or their favour. Whether the presumption applies or not depends on the circumstances of the case. On the one hand if the testator dies so soon after the birth of the child that there was no opportunity to alter, or add to, the will or if the child is born posthumously, it will clearly apply; on the other hand if the testator makes provision for the child by *inter vivos* settlement or in a marriage contract the presumption may not apply.

Confirmation.—Confirmation confers on an executor (or trustee) of the estate of a deceased person power to administer (wind up) the estate. It is obtained by petition to the sheriff of the area in which the deceased had his last **domicile** or, if he had no fixed domicile or was domiciled elsewhere than in Scotland, to the Sheriff of Lothian and Borders. Confirmation ·determines who is to administer the deceased's estate. Before an executor is confirmed he must lodge with the sheriff clerk the deceased's will (if he left one) and an inventory of the deceased's estate which must bear a statement (by the Inland Revenue) that any capital transfer tax payable on it has been settled. (See **Trustee; Domicile.**)

Consistorial action.—Actions relating to the status of husband and wife and of children are consistorial actions. They include actions of declarator of marriage, nullity of marriage, legitimacy, bastardy, divorce, separation, adherence and putting to silence:

the last is designed to prevent a person from maintaining that a child is the legitimate child of another person who denies that the child is his or hers. These actions are for the most part heard in the Court of Session.

Actions for **custody** of, maintenance for, or access to, a child or for payment of sums on or after divorce are not consistorial though they may be dealt with in the course of a consistorial action. These actions are for the most part heard in the sheriff court.

Constructive dismissal.—This is a term used if the employee terminates the **contract of employment** between himself and his employer, with or without notice, where the circumstances entitle him to do so by reason of the employer's conduct. He is entitled to do so if the employer is in breach of such a fundamental term of the contract that he could have been held to have repudiated it. It goes without saying that not all dismissals are unfair. There are rules about the period of notice to be given to terminate employment, the provision of reasons for the termination and the effective date of termination, grounds on which dismissal is to be regarded as fair or unfair, remedies for unfair dismissal (including appeal) to an industrial tribunal, provisions for reinstatement or re-engagement and for compensation for unfair dismissal.

An officer of the Advisory, Conciliation and Arbitration Service (ACAS) will be available to help the employee and the employer to reach a settlement about their rights.

Contempt of court.—This is in the nature of, though not strictly, a crime. It may be committed by disorderly behaviour in court, improper conduct intended to influence the course of justice, or aimed at bringing the administration of justice into disrepute or causing disregard for the authority of the court. Every court has power to punish contempt, and there is an appeal against any punishment imposed.

Contract.—A contract is an agreement intended to be legally enforceable, whereby two or more parties agree to give or do or abstain from doing something for the other's benefit. The subject is vast and textbooks should be consulted.

Contract for services.—See **Contract of employment.**

Contract of employment.—A contract of employment (or of hiring of service as it was called under the old law, and sometimes still is, by lawyers) is that whereby one person, the servant or employee, lets out his services to another, the master or employer, for reward and benefit. The feature which identifies the more usual kind of contract — the contract of service — is that the master or employer is entitled to control the mode in which the required work is to be done, although many employees exercise professional skill or independent judgment and have a large measure of discretion in performing their duties. The less usual contract is the contract for services or for work in which the employee (also the contractor) is employed to perform a function or bring about a result in his own way, both he and the employer relying on the former's own skill and knowledge, there being no detailed control or direction from the employer. Whether a person is employed in the one or the other capacity at a particular time is a question of fact, consideration being given to a number of factors including the work being done. Other relevant factors are the type and manner of remuneration and the power of dismissal. It is also to be noted that the relationship of service and agency may be difficult to distinguish as may also be that of service and partnership. (See also **Service; Vicarious liability**.)

The foregoing is a very general statement of the law of contract of employment. The Employment Protection (Consolidation) Act 1978 (which consolidated the Acts mentioned in the note on **dismissal**) sets out what is virtually a complete code of the law of employment under a contract of service (it does not contain provisions about dismissal of persons employed under contracts for services or certain other employments). It and explanatory pamphlets issued by the Department of Employment should be consulted for more detailed information.

Contract of service.—See **Contract of employment.**

Contributory negligence.—Where one party raises an action of **damages** against another, the latter may plead contributory negligence as a defence. In doing so he is maintaining that the pursuer's carelessness was responsible in some measure for the harm suffered by, or done to, him. The pursuer will, of course, fail in his case if the sole cause of the harm was his own negligence. Contributory negligence results from no more than lack of reasonable care being taken by the pursuer for himself which contributed to the harm he suffered and where this is proved to the court's satisfaction the damages awarded will be reduced accordingly. The Law Reform (Contributory Negligence) Act 1945 may be consulted.

Copyright.—Copyright exists in ideas not in their execution. It existed at **common law** but now only under the Copyright Act 1956. It has been defined, in its most elementary form, as "the right of multiplying copies of a published writing". The Copyright Act 1911 defined it as "the sole right to produce or reproduce the work or any substantial part thereof in any material form whatsoever, to perform or, in the case of a lecture, to deliver the work or any substantial part thereof in public; if the work is unpublished, to publish the work or any substantial part thereof". The 1956 Act extended its scope by providing that it is in relation to a literary, dramatic, musical or artistic work "the exclusive right to do and to authorise other persons to do certain acts in relation to that work". There is copyright in sound recordings, films, broadcasts and in published editions of works there being separate restrictions on the use of each type of work. The Plant Varieties and Seeds Act 1964 introduced copyright in plants. Copyright subsists for 50 years from the end of the year of the author's death or the end of the year in which it was first published if that was after his death.

Copyright, Infringement of.—Copyright of any material is infringed if any person other than the owner makes use of the material. The owner is then entitled to all such relief by way of interdict, damages or otherwise as are available in respect of infringements of other rights in property. Exemplary damages may be awarded in a blatant case.

Corporeal.—See **Moveable Property.**

Corroboration.—Evidence led in support of principal evidence is led in corroboration of it. In Scots law a fact cannot be proved, in the majority of cases, by the testimony of one person alone. That person's evidence must be corroborated by evidence given by another person or by facts and circumstances which amount to corroboration. In actions for damages for personal injuries, if the court is satisfied that any fact has been established by evidence given in the action it has power to find that fact proved even if there is no corroboration of it (see s. 9 of the Law Reform (Miscellaneous Provisions) (Scotland) Act 1968). A number of statutes provide that evidence given in a criminal case by a single witness is sufficient (*e.g.* the Game (Scotland) Act 1832; the Trespass Act 1865).

Counsel.—A counsel is an advocate. All advocates are members of the Faculty of Advocates and may be either junior counsel or, when experienced, senior counsel (Q.C.) appointed by the Queen. Only advocates can draft summonses and other writs initiating actions in the supreme courts — House of Lords, High Court of Justiciary and Court of Session — and are alone entitled to appear in these courts. Counsel frequently also give written opinions on difficult points of law. Counsel may be engaged only through a solicitor.

Count reckoning and payment, action of.—This is an action brought to compel a person to give an account of his dealings (intromissions) with property under his control though not belonging to him and to pay any balance found due to those entitled to it (usually the pursuers). This is particularly the case where the relationship is one of principal and agent and the real question is whether the defender can account for his intromissions.

Counter action (otherwise **Cross action**).—Where a person (the pursuer) raises an action the person against whom it is raised (the defender) is not bound to wait until the pursuer takes steps to proceed with his action but is entitled to raise an action of his own (a counter action) to have his position made clear. There must however be some slight difference between the actions otherwise the defender may not be allowed to proceed because the matter at issue can be decided in full in the pursuer's action. Thus if an ordinary action for the recovery of a sum of money is brought a counter action that no sum is due will not be allowed to proceed. But where, for instance, an action was raised for delivery of an article sold at a public auction, the price of the article being alleged to be the highest made at the auction, a counter action to have it declared that certain bids at the auction were illegal and that the price to be paid was less than that sought was allowed by the court to proceed as a true counter action.

The expression "cross action" is more commonly used in **divorce** proceedings. An action raised by one spouse for divorce may be countered by an action raised by the other, each party maintaining that the other was responsible for the breakdown of the marriage, the grounds alleged by each not being wholly the same.

Court of Appeal.—This is an English expression referring to a court of appellate jurisdiction originally established under s. 1 of the Supreme Court of Judicature (Consolidation) Act 1925 but reconstituted under the Criminal Appeal Act 1966. As is mentioned elsewhere herein, appeals from decisions of the sheriff court in civil cases are heard either by the sheriff principal (see **Sheriff**) or, on choice of the parties, by the Inner House of the Court of Session (see **Court of Session**), and appeals from decisions of the sheriff principal as well as appeals from the Lords Ordinary are also taken by the Inner House. Appeals from Inner House decisions (with a few exceptions) may be made to the House of Lords.

In criminal cases appeals from decisions in all cases under **solemn procedure** are heard by the **Court of Criminal Appeal.**

All these Scottish courts are known colloquially as courts of appeal, but none has that name as its formal title.

Court of Criminal Appeal.—The Criminal Appeal (Scotland) Act 1926 gives a uniform right of appeal to this court — of which three Lords Commissioners of Justiciary form a quorum (see **Lord Justice-General**) — in all criminal cases falling under **solemn procedure.** (For appeals in criminal cases other than those under solemn procedure, see **Appellant**.)

Court of Session.—There are two civil courts in Scotland: the Court of Session, which is the supreme court and sits in Edinburgh; and the sheriff court, which is the local court, there being a sheriff court in most of the main centres of population. The House of Lords is also a court of appeal from decisions of the Court of Session in civil cases. The leading principle of the constitution of the Court of Session is that cases originating in it are decided by judges. The total number of judges (the Senators of the Royal College of Justice) is 21 of whom 13, called **Lords Ordinary** (*q.v.*) deal with cases in the first instance. They sit in what is referred to as the Outer House of the Court of Session. The eight other judges are formed into two divisions of four judges each (three being a quorum) which form the Inner House of the court and which deal with appeals from decisions of the Lords Ordinary, the sheriff court and other matters. The **Lord President** presides over the First Division and the **Lord Justice Clerk** over the Second. A Lord Ordinary may report a case to the Inner House for guidance and the Divisions may consult each other about difficult points of law which arise. In cases of greater difficulty or importance a fuller court, usually seven judges, may be convened and, indeed, the whole court both Inner and Outer Houses may sit as one court in cases of very great difficulty. This is, however, rarely done. Individual judges are not required by law to specialise in specific types of cases, but there are certain types of subject-matter with which the Court of Session alone can deal, such as actions of divorce, declarator of marriage, nullity of marriage, legitimacy, actions for reductions of judicial decrees and **cy-près schemes** (*q.v.*). A wide range of actions may be brought in the sheriff court or the Court of Session, whichever one of the two is chosen by the parties. Included in these are all actions for damages, actions for recovery of debt not exceeding £500, some actions concerning family matters (*e.g.* aliment and custody) and concerning possession of heritable or moveable property.

Court of summary jurisdiction.—A court of summary jurisdiction is a court in which actions both civil and criminal are dealt with by a judge without a jury. The sheriff court is a court of summary jurisdiction although it also has jurisdiction to deal with cases where the procedure is solemn (criminal), *i.e.* the case is dealt with by a jury as well as a judge. The procedure in a **district court** is summary only.

Creditor.—A creditor is a person (natural or legal) to whom another person (the debtor) is indebted (usually in money). A **secured creditor** is one who has been granted a deed by his debtor acknowledging indebtedness and providing security for the sum owed. If the security is heritable property the granting of a standard security is essential; if the security is a corporeal moveable delivery to the creditor is necessary as in the case of pledge (pawn). A creditor may also obtain security for goods sold but not paid for by concluding with his debtor a hire purchase agreement. (See **Warranty.**) Security over incorporeal moveable property may be arranged by assignation of the right to it.

In addition to secured creditors there are creditors having privileged or preferential claims on grounds other than having security for their debts, those with ordinary claims and those with postponed claims. A preferential claim has priority over the others and must be settled before them. This type of claim arises most frequently where the debtor is insolvent. Preferential claims include (where the debtor is deceased) death-bed and funeral expenses and the expenses of winding up the estate. Fees of the trustee in a bankruptcy are also preferred. Following thereon and having common priority are certain rates and taxes, certain wages and salaries, payments due under the National Insurance, the Employment Protection and certain other Acts.

Credit sale.—A credit sale is a sale in which by agreement payment of the price is deferred in whole or in part. *Prima facie* property transfers to a purchaser when the contract is entered into, and the seller has only a personal claim without security for the unpaid price. But in certain cases, as under the Consumer Credit Act 1974, the property remains in the ownership of the seller subject to safeguards for the purchaser.

Croft.—A croft is an agricultural holding of a rather special kind and the law which applies to it, while basically the same as that which applies to other agricultural tenancies, has had a mass of special provisions superimposed on it by the Crofters Holdings (Scotland) Act 1886 (much of which has been repealed) and a series of Acts passed since then, the most recent being the Crofting Reform (Scotland) Act 1976, one of the main provisions of which is that it enables a crofter to purchase the croft of which he is tenant and thus to own it.

An agricultural holding can be a croft only if it is situated in any of the seven **crofting counties** (the same is true of a **statutory small tenancy**), and is one to which, before the passing of the Crofters (Scotland) Act 1955, any of the provisions of the Landholders Acts 1866 to 1931 applied, or a holding in those counties which became a croft by the registration of the tenant as a crofter under the Crofters (Scotland) Act 1955 or a holding which the Secretary of State has directed is to be a croft. Any right in common grazings of the crofting township of which the croft forms part and in which the croft has a share is part of the croft.

Crofting law is difficult to grasp in full even for a lawyer who has worked in its field. One point which requires emphasis is that a crofter who has not purchased the land which forms his croft does not own the croft land or croft house; he is simply the tenant of both and has security of tenure as tenant. He is entitled on ceasing to be tenant (otherwise than by purchase) to compensation for improvements (including the croft house) which he or his predecessors as tenants have made to it. He also has the right to bequeath the tenancy. Information about crofts and crofters' rights law can be obtained from the Crofters Commission, 4/6 Castle Wynd, Inverness (0463-37231).

Crofting counties.—Argyll, Caithness, Inverness, Orkney, Ross and Cromarty, Shetland and Sutherland are the crofting counties.

Cross-examination.—When a **witness** appearing on behalf of one party to an action in court is giving evidence on behalf of that party (and is being questioned by that party or by the lawyer appearing on that party's behalf) the procedure is said to be examination-in-chief of the witness. After the examination-in-chief is completed the other party or his lawyer may then put questions to the witness, and this is described as "cross-examination". After being cross-examined the witness may be re-examined by the party (or his lawyer) on whose behalf he is giving evidence but only to elucidate points already dealt with in the examination or cross-examination. The leading, at this stage, of fresh evidence is not permitted.

Crown.—When the term "the Crown" is used in relation to rights or privileges or any other aspect of Crown interests, it is not the Sovereign that is being referred to but Her Majesty's government. Constitutional lawyers refer to this sometimes as "The Sovereign in Parliament". In theory government ministers and members of staff in their departments are servants of the Sovereign and entitled to the privileges which attach to the Sovereign personally at common law. This theory has been much undermined in recent years by such Acts as the Crown Proceedings Act 1947 and the Law Reform (Miscellaneous Provisions) (Scotland) Act 1966. There is a view that the law of Scotland does not and never did give the same paramount status to the Sovereign as England does. It is frequently a matter of doubt whether a particular person or body is a Crown servant or department of state and thus entitled to the privileged position of the Crown.

Crown Agent.—The Crown Agent is the most senior member of the officials (all of whom are civil servants) who form the staff of the **Crown Office** (*q.v.*) and perform the administrative and executive duties required to enable the law officers to carry out their functions in matters connected with criminal proceedings in the courts and with reports of crimes which are sent to the Crown Office for consideration and for the taking of decisions about action in each case. The Crown Agent (who was in earlier days a solicitor in private practice appointed by and holding office for the same length of time as the Lord Advocate) also acts as solicitor in the unlikely event of the Crown Office or the Lord Advocate's Department becoming involved in a civil action.

Crown Office.—The *Civil Service Year Book* describes the Crown Office as being "responsible for the public prosecution of crime in Scotland" (but see **Crown Agent**). All prosecutions and all appeals against decisions in criminal cases heard in the High Court of Justiciary are conducted by Crown counsel, assisted by Crown Office officials. In the sheriff and district courts prosecutions are conducted by the procurator fiscal service which is administered by the Crown Office. Very recently certain additional functions previously performed by the **Queens and Lord Treasurer's Remembrancer** were transferred to the Crown Office.

Culpa.—Culpa or negligence in the legal sense is the absence of care or inadequate care or diligence taken not to cause or permit harm to persons or not to breach the common law duty to take reasonable care in the particular circumstances. There is an underlying idea, where harm has been caused, of moral blameworthiness which amounts to *culpa* even though it is caused unintentionally.

Curator.—A person below the age of majority (*i.e.* below 18 years of age) normally has a **curator** (in the case of a **pupil** (*q.v.*) called a **tutor**). The father is the natural curator of his legitimate child, but the Guardianship Act 1973 conferred the same right on the mother. The Act should be consulted to find the grounds on which a parent is to act as curator in any particular case. The mother is the curator of her illegitimate child. In either case the court may appoint some other person to be curator if it appears that there is a conflict of interest between the curator and the child or if the curator does not perform his functions.

The function of the curator is not to administer the minor's estate but to give advice on, and consent and concurrence to, the legal actions (*e.g.* sale of property) of the **minor**. Thus, while a minor may himself, without his curator's consent, grant a deed selling or handing over some of his property to another person, the other runs the risk that the minor may resile from the bargain on the grounds that it was to his loss, or, at least, did not confer any benefit on him. A minor must, however, pay for items of food, clothing and other personal necessaries supplied to him.

A curator (called curator *ad litem*) may also be appointed by a court, to act on behalf of a minor in proceedings before the court. A curator may in other circumstances be appointed by the court, *e.g.* to a person who is of unsound mind or who, for any other reason, cannot manage his own affairs. Such a curator is called a *curator bonis* and his function is to manage the whole affairs of the **ward** (the incapacitated person). For this purpose he has the same powers of management as a trustee, but has no power over the ward as a person, *e.g.* he cannot force the ward to live where he, the curator, thinks fit. A curator *ad litem* may also be appointed to conduct a court action on behalf of such a person. (See **Enorm lesion; Quadriennium utile.**)

Custody.—The dictionary meaning of custody is a watching or guarding; care; security; imprisonment. It is used in a number of legal contexts. Parents have custody of their children, although in the case of divorce or separation one of the parents may be awarded custody, or, where parents are neglecting their children, the local authority may take the children into custody.

Again, documents, money, or moveables (*e.g.* jewellery, or title deeds) may be placed in the custody of, say, a bank and, of course, a person who has committed a crime or offence may be taken into custody by the police. (See **Access.**)

Custom.—The **common law** (*q.v.*) embodies many customs which do not require to be proved, because they are accepted as law. In some instances, however, a custom not so recognised may be held to have been accepted by the parties as binding and be treated as authoritative for them. The existence of a custom as law is established if the community accept it as part of the law. To be given this status a custom must be proved by evidence and shown amongst other things to be a definite practice observed in the locality or trade in question but not of necessity throughout Scotland, and not contradictory to the general law (whether common or statutory).

Cy-près scheme.—The *cy-près* principle is part of the law of trusts in its application to public and charitable bequests. Where the intention of the person who creates a **trust** is incapable of being given literal effect or where its literal performance would be unreasonable or in excess of what the law allows, the court will, so as to prevent the trust failing, often settle a scheme which will enable the funds in the trust to be applied *cy-près,* that is, as nearly as may be possible, practicable or reasonable to the intended purpose. The settlement of a *cy-près* scheme is an exercise of the **nobile officium** (*q.v.*) of the Court of Session. The court are asked by the trustees to give effect to a scheme submitted by them in draft (which may be amended by the court). The principle is applicable not only in relation to the objects of the trust but also in relation to the means by which it is to be effected or administered or where the trust purposes have, in fact, failed.

D

Damages.—The word "damages" is used to describe a sum of money claimed (and, on success, payable) as compensation for the loss, injury or damage sustained in consequence of the actings of one person (should the matter reach court that person will normally be the defender), which are in breach of a duty owed, whether by contract or by law, to another person (in court proceedings, the pursuer). There may, of course, be more than one pursuer or one defender. The amount of damages, particularly if awarded in court, is intended, so far as possible, to place the person who receives them, if the other person was wholly responsible for the injury received, in the same or in as good a position as he was before he suffered the loss, or would have been in had he not suffered it, that is to say, in the case for instance of injury as the result of an accident, as if the accident had not occurred or, in the case of loss following on breach of contract, as if there had been no breach. The amount of damages will, however, depend also on a number of factors, including the extent to which the injured party was himself responsible for the occurrence of the loss, injury or damage. (See **Contributory Negligence; Violent profits.**)

Damnum absque injuria means loss or damage suffered without legal wrong.

Damnum fatale.—A Latin phrase much used, but for the most part not in a legal sense. In Scots law it means, shortly put, a loss due to an unusual accident such as the occurrence of an exceptional storm or flood or to circumstances which no human foresight could have provided against. The phrase "act of God" is used to express much the same concept.

Dead's part.—This expression means that part of a person's estate of which he has power to dispose by **will** in any way he wishes. Such part of the estate of a deceased person as is required to meet the **prior** and **legal rights** of a surviving spouse and children is set aside before the "dead's part" can be arrived at.

Declarator.—A declarator is a judicial declaration of a person's rights, made normally at the conclusion of an action before the Inner House of the Court of Session. It declares the pursuer's legal rights but requires nothing further to be done unless, as is usual, other conclusions are annexed. It is decisive not advisory. The pursuer may have a material patrimonial interest in having the rights in question declared to exist.

An action of declarator is the court process by which actings of the Crown (*i.e.* government departments, etc.) can be challenged on grounds, *e.g.* of *vires*. It is not competent for the courts to grant an interdict against the Crown for any purpose (see s. 21 of the Crown Proceedings Act 1947 as interpreted by s. 43), *e.g.* prohibiting an *ultra vires* regulation being given effect. But a decision given in an action of declarator to the effect that a particular action by a government department would be outwith their powers normally results in the action not being taken. (See **Interdict.**)

Decree.—A decree is the term used in Scots law for the judgment of a court in a civil action. It normally orders the loser of the action to do something (*e.g.* where the successful party is seeking to obtain a sum of money from the other, the decree will find the sum to be due and order the other party to pay it) or, of course, will exonerate the defender from doing, paying or submitting to anything if the court finds that the pursuer has not proved his case. In important cases there will be appended to the decree itself a note or statement, by one, some or all of the judges who heard the case, setting out the reasons for reaching the conclusion that the decree should, or should not, be granted. An extract of a decree must be obtained to enable it to be enforced.

De die in diem.—From day to day. This is one way in which the law requires the passage of time to be computed; another way is from minute to minute — *de momento in momentum.*

Deed of arrangement.—A deed of arrangement is most commonly entered into in the context of **bankruptcy.** After the court has awarded a **sequestration** on a petition being made to them, meetings of the bankrupt's creditors are held. At the first meeting (which the Bankruptcy Act 1913 requires to be held for the election of a trustee) a majority in number and three-fourths in value of the creditors present or represented may decide that the estate ought to be wound up under such a deed and that an application be made to the court to **sist** (*q.v.*) sequestration procedure. The creditors may at any time, while the sist continues, present to the court a deed of arrangement. The court may approve the deed and declare the sequestration at an end; the debtor's estate may be ingathered and distributed either by the creditors or by a trustee as the deed provides. The deed may also provide that, if the bankrupt pays a fixed sum, his estate will be restored to him, and may also provide for his discharge.

A deed of arrangement of a different kind may be entered into by the beneficiaries of an estate of a deceased person where there is dispute about the manner in which property comprised in the estate should be distributed. It is simply a contract between all the beneficiaries and, if properly authenticated by all of them by signature, is binding on each, and the estate will be distributed accordingly.

De facto.—A matter of fact or a fact established.

Defamation.—Defamation is the malicious communication to others concerning a person, in words or by innuendo, of a concept which is false in fact and discrediting in its nature, injurious to his feelings or damaging to his reputation. "Slander" and "libel" are, in Scots law simply other words for defamation. (In English law they have different meanings.) Whether or not the view expressed is defamatory is a matter of law. The person who is defamed has a right of action for damages, but where a statement is made about a class or group each one of the members of it has a right of action only if what is said applies to him personally so as to affect his reputation. To say, for instance, that all lawyers are thieves does not, even if it is untrue, confer a right of damages on individual lawyers.

Defender.—The defender is the person against whom a pursuer raises a **civil action** in court. (The English term is "defendant".) It is seldom used to refer to the person against whom criminal action is taken, that person being known as "the accused" or, after he has been before the court, "the **panel**" (*q.v.*).

Deferred sentence.—A court which is trying a criminal case has power to adjourn the hearing of the case, and this is declared by statute to include power — after a person has been convicted or the court has found that he has committed the offence but before he is sentenced — to adjourn the case to enable inquiries to be made or to decide on the most suitable method of dealing with the case. The court must not, however, for such purpose adjourn the hearing of, and defer giving sentence on, the case for any single period exceeding three weeks.

Delict.—A delict is the conduct, whether deliberate or negligent and whether by act or omission, of a person in breach of a legal duty imposed by law as the result of which some other person has suffered hurt or loss or harm. It is not necessarily a criminal act or omission, although the conduct may have criminal as well as civil consequences. The person who committed the delict has an obligation in law to make reparation (*e.g.* pay a sum by way of damages or restore damaged property to its former condition if that is possible) to the person who suffered from it. An instance of the sort of conduct envisaged is reckless or careless driving of a motor car which results in a collision with another car and causes damage to that car or injury to its occupants.

De momento in momentum.—See **De die in diem.**

De novo.—Anew or afresh. To begin again in the discussion or hearing of a cause.

Deportation order.—The Home Office, who have general control of aliens (see **Alien**) in this country have power to make an order requiring an alien to leave the UK and thereafter to remain out of the country. (The Scottish Office has no official function in the matter.) The order is known as a deportation order and there are two situations in which it may be made.

Deposit receipt.—This is not a legal term; it is the acknowledgement which a Scottish bank gives that money has been deposited with them. The money may be uplifted by (repaid to) the depositor at any time simply by his endorsing the receipt. If the money has been in the hands of the bank for longer than one month, interest is paid for each complete month.

Designation.—This word has no specifically legal meaning. It is used, of course, by lawyers and by others as meaning a person's name, title (if he has one), appellation, description of occupation, standing etc., and the address at which he is living or has his permanent abode.

Detention.—A person between 16 and 21 years of age who is convicted of an offence, punishable in the case of a person over 21 years by imprisonment, may be sentenced to be detained in such a place and on such conditions as the Secretary of State may direct. Sections 41 to 45 of the Criminal Justice (Scotland) Act 1980 contain an up-to-date code relating to detention.

Diet.—This word is used in relation to criminal proceedings in court and means simply a meeting of the court for the purpose of taking steps in the proceedings in any prosecution. (It is also used loosely to mean a date on which the court is to meet).

There are in every criminal proceeding, except one to which s. 12 of the Criminal Justice (Scotland) Act 1980 applies, two diets with possible continuations of the second in every criminal cause. The first takes place in the sheriff court, the second may also take place there, or may be in the High Court of Justiciary, depending on the gravity of the crime or offence. At the first or pleading diet the accused states whether he intends to plead guilty or not guilty. The main reason for having a pleading diet is to avoid unnecessary expense in citing and securing the attendance of witnesses and jurors. If there is to be a trial it takes place at the second diet which cannot be held earlier than nine clear days after the first diet and may be held much later if continuations are allowed so that, for instance, further inquiries may be made. A trial diet may also be abandoned.

The notice of a first and second diet in the sheriff court must be in the form set out in Schedule F to the Criminal Procedure (Scotland) Act 1887. A second form (Schedule G to that Act) deals with the second diet in the High Court as well as the first diet in the sheriff court. Further provisions about the first diet appear in ss. 59-77 and 102-111 of the Criminal Procedure (Scotland) Act 1975. An accused who fails to attend any diet may be fined if no excuse for the failure is available.

Diligence.—Diligence is, most commonly, the term used to describe the legal procedure by which the person to whom money is owed (the creditor) takes steps to ensure that the person who owes the money (the debtor) either —

(i) will appear in court to answer, if he has any answer to make, to an action for payment raised by the creditor;

(ii) will give the creditor security, in advance of a decree being given by the court, for the amount of the sum which the court may ultimately find that the debtor owes; and

(iii) will implement a decree already given by the court.

The diligence available to creditors is not the only form of diligence. The service of a summons is a preliminary to diligence, from it the pursuer may proceed (*e.g.* to arrestment on the dependence) (see **Arrestment**).

Diminished responsibility.—This is a defence available to an accused person who has been charged with a crime. It has existed in Scots law for over a century but is difficult to understand and has never been fully defined. Lord Alness said of it: "It is very difficult to put it in a phrase, but it has been put in this way: that there must be aberration or weakness of mind; that there must be some form of mental unsoundness; that there must be a state of mind which is bordering on, though not amounting to, insanity; that there must be a mind so affected that responsibility is diminished from full responsibility to partial responsibility — in other words, the prisoner in question must be only partially accountable for his actions. And I think I can see running through the cases that there is implied . . . that there must be some form of mental disease" (*H.M. Advocate* v. *Savage, 1923 J.C. 49* at p. 51).

Dismissal.—An employee is, for the purpose of the rules of unfair dismissal to which Pt. V of the Employment Protection (Consolidation) Act 1978 gives effect, treated as having been dismissed if (a) the contract under which he is employed (written or oral, expressed or implied) is terminated by the employer whether with or without notice; or (b) where the contract is for a fixed period of time (fixed term contract) that term expires without being renewed under the same contract (see **Contract of Employment; Constructive Dismissal**).

Dispone.—Used in relation to land, this word means to transfer ownership. It was formerly essential to use the word to give validity to any deed transferring ownership of land.

Disposition.—A contract for the sale of heritable property (*e.g.* land, buildings, etc.) is given effect to, and title to the land in most instances transferred by, a formal document called a disposition. A disposition, though usually in implement following on a sale, may be granted by the owner of a property in other circumstances, *e.g.* on **sequestration** (*q.v.*) or even gratuitously "for love, favour and affection". On delivery to the purchaser (disponee) it supersedes all earlier communings relating to the particular transaction.

The form of the disposition for the most part still follows that set out in the Titles to Land Consolidation (Scotland) Act 1868, which has, however, been much amended. It contains clauses narrating the sale, the transfer of the property, the date at which the buyer is to get actual possession, the feudal conditions applicable (by reference, if necessary to other deeds containing them) and there are a number of other clauses of a more technical nature to which statutes have given meaning. It is to be remembered that all but small areas of the land and buildings in Scotland were, and in theory still are, subject to the feudal system of land tenure, and much that appears in a disposition (unless it be of very recent date) cannot be fully understood unless the theory and practice of the system are first understood.

Much of that system was altered by Acts of Parliament passed in the late nineteenth century. In very recent years (1970 and 1974) further far-reaching alterations were made to it. Two of the most important of these are that variation or discharge of the feudal conditions applicable to any property (*e.g.* that it will be used only as a dwelling-house) may be sought by application to the **Lands Tribunal for Scotland,** and that the ownership of property for which a feuduty is payable cannot now be transferred by the owner until the feuduty is redeemed. **Stamp duty** is paid on a disposition if the price or value exceeds £20,000.

Disqualification.—This word is used most frequently in the context of road traffic offences. If a person is found guilty of driving or attempting to drive a motor vehicle on a road or other public place with more than the prescribed limit of alcohol in his blood the judge must disqualify him from holding or obtaining a driving licence for one year at least if it is his first offence, or three years if he has been convicted within the previous ten years of that and any other offence for which he was disqualified. If a person drives a vehicle while he is disqualified a further period of disqualification may be imposed. The same provisions apply in the case of a person who is unfit to drive while under the influence of drugs, except that the breath test applies only in the case of drink. The Road Traffic Acts 1960 and 1972 should be consulted (see also **Breath test; Blood test; Urine test**).

Dissolution of marriage.—There are a number of circumstances in which a marriage may be dissolved, the commonest being the death of one of the parties, divorce or **declarator** of **nullity** of the marriage.

District court.—The District Courts (Scotland) Act 1975 abolished all the justice of the peace courts, quarter sessions, burgh courts and the Court of the Bailie of the River and Firth of Clyde which had existed before 16 May 1975 and created district courts in their place. The Act provides for a district court to be in each district or islands area within the meaning of the Local Government (Scotland) Act 1973 and, but for one or two areas, a court now exists in each.

District courts have jurisdiction in the same matters (with one or two exceptions) as the courts they have replaced and also those of burgh magistrates, judges of police and justices of the peace when acting as courts of summary jurisdiction. Their jurisdiction is broadly in less important criminal cases (*e.g.* breach of the peace) and their members are not legally qualified except where the court consists of a stipendiary magistrate who also has the additional summary criminal jurisdiction and powers of a sheriff. (See **Stipendiary magistrate.**)

Divorce.—Divorce is one of the means by which a marriage may be dissolved (see **Dissolution of marriage** for others), the spouses being divorced from each other on the ground that the marriage has broken down irretrievably. Only the Court of Session has power to grant a divorce in Scotland. Irretrievable breakdown is taken to be established (see s. 1 (2) of the Divorce (Scotland) Act 1976) if the defender has committed adultery, cruelty, or has deserted the pursuer. The court may also grant decree of divorce where there has been absence of cohabitation for two years and the defender consents to the granting of decree, or there has been absence of cohabitation for five years even if the defender does not consent.

Docquet.—A summary of a longer writing. Originally it was used almost exclusively in relation to an instrument of sasine, a deed which formerly was an essential feature of feudal tenure.

Domicile.—In law the word "domicile" does not necessarily mean the place where a person lives. No person can, however, be without a domicile and a person can have only one domicile at any particular time. (Some legal systems admit the possible existence of more than one domicile.) A person's domicile is the state, territory or country which is regarded as his or her permanent home. Every person has a domicile of origin which he will have acquired from his parents (or parent if only one is known) but, after he attains majority or is **forisfamiliated** (*q.v.*) he can acquire a domicile for himself. Scots law has rules for deciding for its own purposes where a person is domiciled but not all legal systems have the same rules for this purpose.

Dominant tenement.—This expression refers to the land, buildings or other subjects the title to which includes a right to exercise a **servitude** (*e.g.* a right of access, a right to receive daylight, a right to a water supply) over or from neighbouring land. The property over or out of which the servitude is exercised is called the **servient tenement** (*q.v.*).

Donation inter vivos.—This expression means simply a gift made by one person to another both of whom are living and in their right minds, the intention being to transfer rights of ownership gratuitously. The gift can be made in many ways. In the case of **corporeal moveable property** it is usually made by delivery of the gift by the donor to the donee. There are, however, exceptions to this generality. Thus, while money in the form of notes or coins can be donated by mere delivery, the delivery of a share certificate, a cheque or a deposit receipt is, in itself, not sufficient evidence of the intention to donate the value of the shares, the amount of the cheque or in the deposit receipt unless delivery is accompanied by a written expression of intention to donate. Where the gift is of **incorporeal moveables** or of heritable property, it is enforceable only if it is made by a written deed. If the transaction does not take immediate effect the intention to make a gift is put in doubt. There is a legal presumption against donation.

Donation mortis causa.—A donation *mortis causa* is a gift made in contemplation of death though not necessarily in the belief that death is by reason of illness or other cause imminent. The gift may be made by delivery in the presence of a witness or by deed so that the right of property which is being gifted is immediately transferred to the donee. Such a donation is however only a qualified one being subject to the condition that if the donee predeceases the donor the gift reverts to the donor who may revoke the gift (on recovery from the illness which prompted the making of the gift). The property gifted, or the document of title to it must, normally, be delivered to the donee or to someone on his behalf. The donation is effective on the death of the donor.

As in the case of donation *inter vivos* there is a presumption against donation and there must therefore always be evidence of the intention to donate. The making of such a donation, though similar, is not identical with the provision by testamentary writing for payment of a legacy. It differs from a legacy in not requiring writing and in several other respects, but is the same as a legacy in being revocable and in certain other respects such as the absence of effect on **legal rights** and liability to meet debts of the donor.

The question of whether a gift has or has not been made has arisen most frequently in connection with money lying on **deposit receipt.** A deposit receipt in the donor's name may be donated *mortis causa* by endorsement and delivery to the donee. If it is in the donee's name or in joint names of donor and donee or in their joint names and the survivor of them, it is, except in certain circumstances, indicative of intention by the person who placed it on deposit to make a gift of it to the other person.

Duress.—Duress is of importance in the law of contract. The dictionary meaning of the word is constraint illegally exercised to force a person by threats or otherwise to perform some act. The threats need not be of physical violence but they may be, for example, ones to kill the person himself or a near relative or of disgrace or financial ruin and they must, it is clear, be illegal or unjustifiable. If a person is induced to enter into a contract or agreement under duress, he can raise an action in court to have the contract or agreement declared **void** and have it reduced. The duress must be of such a degree as would overcome the fortitude of a reasonable man or woman.

Duty solicitor.—A duty solicitor has the functions set out in Article 6 of the Legal Aid (Scotland) (Criminal Proceedings) Scheme 1964. Principally he is available to attend on persons in custody on a charge of murder or culpable homicide, to give legal aid to persons appearing in front of the sheriff on petition on solemn procedure (see **indictment**) or who are in custody on their first appearance before the sheriff on summary complaint.

The duty solicitor is one of a number of solicitors named in the duty plan which every local legal aid committee is required to prepare annually. It provides that a duty solicitor will be available at the sheriff court of the area on court days at all times throughout the year. A copy of the plan is in the hands of the chief constable in the area of the local committee and the sheriff in that area has a copy. It can be seen on request.

E

Edinburgh Gazette.—The *Edinburgh Gazette* is the official publication of the Government in Scotland and is registered as a newspaper. Notices in it are evidence of acts of state and of everything done by the Sovereign in her political capacity. Provisions in numerous statutes require notice of certain events or steps taken in proceedings to be advertised in the *Gazette*. It is printed for Her Majesty's Stationery Office and is on sale at any H.M.S.O. shop.

EEC Instruments.—The framework of the policies of the European Economic Community is contained in three main treaties, namely the EEC Treaty (or Treaty of Rome) of 1957, the ECSC (European Coal and Steel Community) Treaty (1952) and the Euratom Treaty (1957). They constitute the "Primary EEC legislation". The EEC Treaty does not cover the whole field of law. What it does cover are, broadly, customs duties, agriculture, free movement of labour, services and capital, transport, monopolies and restrictive practices and state aid for industry. To give effect to those policies the institutions of the Communities (the Council of Ministers and the Commission) make detailed implementing instruments known as "Community Secondary Legislation". The annual number of such instruments runs into thousands and about 70 per cent are concerned with short-lived changes in the rate of levy or support payments on agriculture products. The more important instruments are made by the Council of Ministers after draft proposals have been put forward to them by the Commission; the Commission makes instruments only under powers delegated to it by the Council for minor or consequential matters. The instruments are of three main types:

(1) *EEC Regulations*. These are the most common, are of general application and have direct and binding effect as law in the legal systems of each of the member states. The UK entered the Community by means of the European Community Act 1972 which made the legislative changes necessary for the purpose. All EEC Regulations thus apply in Scotland directly, no further implementary legislation being needed to give them legal effect. They take precedence over the law of Scotland in the same field as that with which they are concerned;

(2) *EEC Directives*. These are binding on each member state as to the results they seek to achieve but it is left to each member state to decide how to implement them. This means that, so far as Scotland is concerned, Parliament must amend Scots law or Scots practice must be altered to bring the one or the other into line with Community law; and

(3) *EEC Decisions*. These are not of general application throughout the Community, but are addressed either to one of the Member States or to an undertaking or individual within a state, and are designed to bring the law of a Member State or the practice of the undertaking or individual into line with Community law or practice.

Effeiring.—In ordinary usage, to appertain or to relate to. Used in the phrase "effeiring to" it normally refers to ancilliary rights which, though not part of heritable property being conveyed, pertain to and are transferred with it.

Eik.—An eik is an addition made by an executor to the inventory of an estate he is administering. Its object is to include in the confirmation and thus confer power on him to administer items of property which were omitted in error from the original inventory.

Ejection and **Removing.**—An action of ejection is raised against a person who is occupying premises of any kind which he has not, and never had, any title to occupy. An action of removing is raised against a person occupying premises of which he has a right, or a disputed right, to occupy. In either the action is raised because the occupant refuses to vacate the premises.

Ejusdem generis.—Literally "of the same kind or nature". Where in a statute or deed particular classes are specified by name followed by general words, the general words are taken, generally, to apply to those *ejusdem generis* with the particular classes.

Endorsement of driving licence.—Where a person is found guilty and convicted of certain offences under road traffic legislation, the court which convicts him is obliged to order that particulars of the conviction and, if the court orders him to be disqualified from driving, particulars of the disqualification are to be endorsed on any driving licence held by him. Such an endorsement can be used as evidence of the conviction or disqualification.

Enorm lesion.—See **Lesion enorm.**

Entail.—An entail was a **disposition** of heritable property to a prescribed line of heirs. The disposition contained a number of clauses with rather special provisions, some prohibiting alienation of any part of the property conveyed, the borrowing of money on security of the property and the alteration (usually prohibition) of the order in which the heirs were to succeed to the property. If any prohibited act was done, the disposition not only usually annulled it but the heir of entail who was responsible for so acting usually forfeited his right to the property. Entails were first authorised in 1685 but the creation of new entails has been prohibited since 1914.

Estate.—The estate of a person is all that he owns, both heritable and moveable. In many cases it is combined with the word "means", *i.e.* means and estate. In a more limited sense it refers to land owned by a person as in the phrase "landed estate".

Esto.—This is used in the sense of "Be it that so-and-so is the fact or position" or "Given that such-and-such is the fact, position or case" then something else will, it can be argued, follow.

Evidence.—Evidence is used as a means of proving an unknown or disputed fact. In a court action it has the wider meaning of the information made available to the court. There are many specialties in this field, some deriving from common law (see for instance **hearsay evidence**), most from statute (see ss. 26-32 of the Criminal Justice (Scotland) Act 1980, which deals with evidence in criminal trials).

Ex facie.—The phrase means roughly "on the face of it". Given that for example such-and-such a statement has been, at first sight, correctly made or bears out what is being argued for, then the argument or case can proceed on the assumption that it is correct unless or until the contrary is established.

Excambion.—By a contract of excambion one area or description of land is exchanged for another. The word itself thus means simply exchange of lands.

Executor.—An executor is the legal personal representative of a deceased person (but he is not the same as a trustee). His function is to administer (*i.e.* ingather and distribute) the deceased's estate, of which he becomes the nominal owner for the purpose. He pays the deceased's debts, death bed and funeral expenses, capital transfer and other taxes, settles the rights of the deceased's relatives to their share of the estate and disposes of the remainder, if there is any, in accordance with the deceased's will if he leaves one. He pays legacies left by the will, and makes over the **residuary estate** (*q.v.*) to those to whom it is left. If the deceased does not leave a will the executor will distribute the estate in accordance with the rules of intestate succession. Where there is a will and an executor (or executors) is nominated in it, he or she is called an *executor nominate;* where there is no will, or if the person nominated predeceases or refuses to take up office, the sheriff, on being petitioned for the purpose, will appoint an executor and an executor so appointed is called an *executor dative.* The executor is also responsible for disposing of the deceased's body by cremation, burial or otherwise as may be decided by the deceased's relatives, the deceased's wishes, if any, expressed orally or in writing being taken into account. An executor cannot take any steps in connection with the deceased's estate until he has obtained **confirmation** (*q.v.*). His liability is limited to the extent of the estate of the deceased and he cannot be required to pay any of the deceased's debts out of his own means. He is not paid for his work, unless the will so provides but he may be left, and can accept, a legacy under the deceased's will. (See also **Trustees; Residue.**)

Executor dative.—See **Executor.**

Executor nominate.—See **Executor.**

Ex facie absolute disposition.—Until the passing of the Conveyancing and Feudal Reform (Scotland) Act 1970 which introduced the **standard security,** it was not uncommon for a person who owned heritable property and wished to borrow money to grant as security for the loan an absolute disposition of the property in favour of the lender. Though the disposition was in terms *ex facie* absolute and not redeemable, the intention was that the disponee (creditor) should hold the property in security only. This was normal practice where the lender was a building society. The title was taken in the society's name but an agreement (back letter) was granted setting out the true position. Section 9 (3) of the 1970 Act, however, did away with this form of security and s. 40 provides a form for the discharge of such as existed in 1970. (See **Standard Security; Foreclosure.**)

Ex gratia.—Translated into slang terms this means "for free". Something — money, goods, land or any other property or thing — is made over *ex gratia* by the owner to another without expectation of or demand for any payment or other return for it.

Ex hypothesi.—A statement made as a theory, usually for the sake of argument is said to be made *ex hypothesi*.

Ex officio.—A person who holds an appointment or office may, by virtue of his holding that position, also hold some other public or private position. One of the perquisites of holding the appointment or office may be that he is entitled to be invited to attend formal associated functions.

Ex parte.—An *ex parte* statement is a statement made by one side only in proceedings in court or before a tribunal; they are *ex parte* in most instances because the person against whom they are brought is not heard. The phrase means roughly of the one part or one-sided. Thus an *ex parte* statement is a statement of one side only. With a few exceptions, a court or tribunal cannot pronounce a decision unless both parties have had an opportunity of making submissions and arguments on the matter in dispute. Where a court or tribunal gives a decision without hearing both parties, it is said to have acted in a way contrary to **natural justice** and the decision can be reduced.

An instance of proceedings in which an *ex parte* statement is sufficient to enable the court to authorise steps to be taken is **interdict** (*q.v.*). Where a person asks the court to prevent another from taking some action he may apply to the court for interim interdict, and if the court is satisfied from his statement that there are grounds for supposing the action will be taken but should not be permitted until the court have the full facts before them and have reached a final decision, interim interdict will be granted. Thereafter of course, a full hearing will be held before the final decision is given.

Expede.—To draw up, make out, complete a deed, *e.g.* a will or disposition.

Ex post facto.—After the event. When a statement is made about an event which has already happened it is made *ex post facto*. Something done so as to affect another thing done before.

Ex proprio motu.—This Latin phrase roughly translated means "on his own" or "without prompting or being moved by a party to do the thing".

Extract.—In Scots law this means a formal copy of a legal document, as for example a copy of a decree of court extracted from the court records which can be used by the party in whose favour the decree is granted to take further steps to enforce it against the defender. The copy must be certified as a true one.

F

Fair comment.—In an action for damages for defamation based on comment made on facts, it is a defence that the comment was fair. The facts must be substantially true and truly stated; the comment must be fairly and honestly made and must be on a matter of public interest. To be fair the comment must be the honest expression of a view held in good faith but not necessarily moderate, temperate or restrained, though it must not be malicious or simply abuse or invective. Matters of public interest include the conduct of government, both central and local, matters associated with proceedings, decisions of public bodies and institutions, public entertainments and performances (see **Defamation**).

Fatal accident inquiries.—The Fatal Accidents and Sudden Deaths Inquiry (Scotland) Act 1976 (which replaced and repealed the Fatal Accidents Inquiry (Scotland) Act 1895 and the Act of 1906 of the same name) contains provisions about the case of a death which appears to have resulted from an accident occurring in Scotland while the deceased was engaged in his employment, or was in legal custody, or in the case of a death in which it appears to the Lord Advocate that an inquiry should be held into the circumstances of the death on the ground that it was sudden, suspicious, or unexplained or that its occurrence gives rise to serious public concern. The Act provides that in any such case the procurator fiscal of the district with which the circumstances of the death appear to be most closely connected is to investigate those circumstances (usually with the help of the police) and thereafter to apply to the sheriff of the area for the holding of a public inquiry. It is of importance to notice that, although he is required to make a finding about certain aspects of the circumstances surrounding the death, the sheriff has no power to find that any particular person is responsible for its occurrence. And no finding of the sheriff may be used in any other judicial proceedings, *e.g.* in an action for damages raised after the inquiry by relatives of the deceased the findings cannot be made use of. Notice of these inquiries is given in the press.

Fee.—The full right of property in subjects of which a **liferent** (*q.v.*) has been conferred, usually by a testamentary writing on some person other than the **fiar**.

Feu.—A feu is, in modern terms, an area of land (on which a building may or may not have been built) owned and possessed by a person (known as the "Feuar" or "Vassal"), who holds it on feudal tenure. The deeds or writs which form the title to a feu (*e.g.* feu charter, feu contract, feu disposition, or, simply, disposition) will set out the conditions under which the feu is held. One such condition, which appears in most titles granted before 1974, required the vassal to pay a feuduty (or perpetual rent) to the person who, for the time being, owned or owns what is known as the "superiority" of the feu (that person being known as the "superior" — in theory the ultimate superior of all except **udal** land is the Crown). The Land Tenure Reform (Scotland) Act

1974 prohibits the creation of new feuduties, confers on a vassal the right to redeem his feuduty at any term of Whitsunday (15 May) or Martinmas (11 November) on payment of the statutory redemption money, and provides for compulsory redemption of feuduty when land is sold. Conditions about the kind of use to which the land feued and building erected on it may be put are also usual, and other conditions may now be varied or discharged. The Conveyancing and Feudal Reform (Scotland) Act 1970 contains provisions about such variations and discharges and about allocation of feuduties.

Feuar.—See **Feu.**

Feuduty.—See **Feu.**

Fiar.—This word is used primarily in relation to heritable property which is subject to liferent. A proper liferent is the right conferred usually by **testamentary writing** (*q.v.*) to possess, use and enjoy subjects during the grantee's (*i.e.* the liferenter's) lifetime (see **Liferent**). The **fee** (q.v.) of the liferented subjects is vested in another person known as the fiar to whom the rights of actual possession, use and enjoyment revert on the expiry of the liferent. The question whether the bequest of heritage is one of liferent or fee depends on the granter's intention, but the wording of the deed by which the bequest is made may raise doubts about the intention. There are rules about the extent of the fiar's and liferenter's rights and duties in relation to the liferented property so long as the liferent subsists.

Fiduciary.—(the "c" is soft in pronunciation.) Scots law uses this word to denote property held in trust or in the nature of a trust. An instance of its use is to be found in the case of property which is liferented. The right to the property when the liferent comes to an end (*e.g.* on the death of the liferenter) is a right to the fee of the property and the trust comes to an end also.

Fixtures and fittings.—Where a thing by itself moveable is connected with **heritage** (*q.v.*) a question may arise whether it remains moveable (thus termed a fitting) or has become so much a part of the heritage as to be regarded as a fixture, *i.e.* not removable. The question arises probably most frequently in connection with dwelling houses. Things so annexed or adapted that they cannot be removed without destruction of, or damage to, the dwelling house are fixtures, *e.g.* sinks, baths, some kinds of shelving and accessories to heating installations, *e.g.* an oil tank. Examples of fittings are curtain rails, electric bulbs and most gas and electric appliances.

Floating charge.—The Companies (Floating Charges and Receivers) (Scotland) Act 1972 enables a company, in order to create by way of a floating charge security for any debt, debentures or other obligation incurred or to be incurred by or binding on the company, to create a floating charge in favour of the creditor or a trustee for debenture holders. This is done by the company executing under its seal, or by an attorney authorised for the purpose by the company executing an instrument of charge over all or any part of the company's property (including uncalled capital) which is or may be in their hands while the instrument is in force. This is a very brief statement of the position; the Act should be consulted.

Foreclosure.—A person who has loaned money to the owner of heritable property which has been conveyed to him in security of the loan will probably at some time wish to obtain repayment of the money. If all other means of obtaining repayment fail, there remains the procedure of foreclosure. The procedure which is complicated cannot be set out in detail here. The following is a very brief statement of it. Since 1970 with the passing of the Conveyancing and Feudal Reform (Scotland) Act 1970 (which was amended by the Redemption of Standard Securities (Scotland) Act 1971), the granting of a standard security has become the only method by which the owner of heritable property can obtain a loan (mortgage) over the property, reserving to himself a right to redeem the security. (A mortgage — which is properly an English term — may also still exist by the granting of an *ex facie* absolute disposition, *i.e.* a disposition granted by the owner of the property — not the borrower — directly to the lender.)

The creditor serves a notice of default on the debtor in a prescribed form. If he does not comply with the notice the creditor may proceed to exercise such of the rights conferred on him by s. 10 of the 1970 Act as he thinks fit. One of these is a right to sell the property after advertisement. If this fails to effect a sale or if the price obtained is less than the amount due under the security, the creditor can apply to the court for decree of foreclosure. After there is served on (sent to) the debtor intimation of the application and such other intimations and things are done as the court orders, the decree of foreclosure is granted.

The decree contains a declaration that, on an extract of it being recorded in the **Register of Sasines,** any right of redemption by the debtor has been extinguished. The creditor then has right to the property, and also has the same right as the debtor to redeem any security ranking before or on equal terms with his own. Even if decree is granted, any personal obligation of the debtor remains in force in so far as not clearly extinguished.

Foreshore.—See **Regalia minora.**

Forisfamiliation.—This is the departure of a child who is a minor (very exceptionally a pupil) from the family on setting up on his or her own account or marrying. A minor child who has been forisfamiliated does not in strict law require to have a curator to consent to his actings.

Functions.—This word means, in relation to any office of which a person is the holder or to any corporation or other body, the powers conferred and duties imposed on him, or it, by statute or which he, or it, is otherwise entitled, or required by law, to exercise.

Fund in medio.—In an action of **multiplepoinding** where there are several claimants to the property the ownership of which is in dispute, the property is referred to as the fund *in medio.*

Furthcoming, action of (also **Forthcoming**).—Where a party to an action is granted a decree for payment of a sum of money in cash or other property and it is known or believed by him that money or property belonging to the defender is in the hands of a third party (*e.g.* a bank), the third party being called "the

42

arrestee", and the defender or party against whom the decree is granted "the common debtor", then, if the person against whom the decree has been granted makes no arrangement to pay the sum due, the creditor's first step is to arrest the cash or property. Arrestment, however, merely prevents the arrestee from giving up possession of the property, although the debtor may by formal action authorise the arrestee to make over the property to the creditor. If this course is not followed the creditor can raise an action of furthcoming in which the court may order the property to be handed to the creditor.

G

Grassum.—A grassum is a single payment made in addition to a periodic payment such as rent or feuduty. Its use has been extended in recent years to other payments as, for instance, one made to the landlord of a house by a person who wishes to obtain the tenancy of it. It is made usually in exchange for the key of the house.

Great Britain.—Scotland and England and Wales comprise Great Britain.

Ground annual.—A ground annual was (and is) a payment made annually in perpetuity. It is created by a contract entered into as a substitute for, or in addition to, a feu contract. It is made in respect of land described in the contract and was (and is) a real burden. It was found particularly where land could not be sub-feued (*e.g.* entailed land) and where as a result no perpetual annual payment of feuduty for the land could be provided for. The law relating to ground annuals was and is similar to that relating to feuduties. The creation of ground annuals in future is thus prohibited and their allocation and redemption are provided for in the Conveyancing and Feudal Reform (Scotland) Act 1970 and the Land Tenure Reform (Scotland) Act 1974 in the same way as the creation, allocation and redemption of feuduties are provided for in these Acts.

Guarantee.—In the strict sense a guarantee is similar to a cautionary obligation (see **Caution**). It is what one man obliges himself in writing to do to ensure performance of something by another who is the proper and primary party. It is a promise to answer for the debt or default of another. It also can mean the responsibility one person assumes for the truth of a statement made by another. Perhaps its commonest use now is the undertaking given to the buyer of goods by the manufacturer or retailer of them.

Guardian.—The word "guardian" in Scotland is a compendium and has no specific meaning. It covers parents, tutors, curators and other persons having **custody** of a child and therefore parental functions to perform in relation to the child. Thus the differing powers which are exercised by the holders of these offices have to be looked at. Many of these powers are derived from the common law of Scotland, but there has been a series of statutes (virtually all of which use English terms and have English law as

43

their foundation) dealing with them.

The earliest of these Acts is the Guardianship of Infants Act 1886 and there have been numerous statutes since, the most recent being Part II of the Guardianship Act 1973. The principal aim of the 1973 Act was to confer on the mother the same powers as the father in relation to the child. It provides that the rights and authority of mother and father are to be equal and to be exercisable without the other. If they disagree either may apply to the Court of Session which deals with the matters relating to custody and access by virtue of the **nobile officium** or to the sheriff.

The powers and authority of a "guardian" can be dealt with here only briefly. They are of two kinds, that of guiding and directing the persons of children under full age and that of legal administration, that is, managing and advising on the management of the property and legal business of the child so long as the child is a pupil. The powers end fully when majority is attained at 18 years of age.

The Acts (the collective name of which is the Guardianship of Children (Scotland) Acts 1886 to 1973) provide that, so far as custody, upbringing, administration of property and application of income are concerned, the court (if the matter comes before them) must regard the welfare of the child as the paramount consideration. Each parent has a right of custody, and, if the circumstances so warrant, some other person may be appointed as **tutor** (*q.v.*) (The Custody of Children (Scotland) Act 1939 should be looked at for provision about the custody, maintenance, education of and access to children under 16.) The Acts also make it possible for application to be made to the court for the removal of a tutor (even if it be a parent), the appointment of a **judicial factor** (*q.v.*) *loco tutoris* (in place of a tutor), and for either parent to appoint a tutor to his or her pupil child in his or her will.

The main function of a curator is, on the other hand, to give consent to actings of the minor who may, for instance, dispose of his own property with the consent of his curator. If the minor is being maintained and educated at the expense of the curator, it is manifest that the latter will in practice have some control over the minor's person and expenditure. The minor, may, of course, leave the parental home, and thus being **forisfamiliated** (q.v.) can manage his own affairs without parental interference. (See also **Access; Curator; Quadriennium utile; Tutor.**)

H

Haver.—(pronounce as in "have"). A person having in his possession documents or other things which he is required to produce as evidence in legal proceedings.

Health Service Commissioner.—The Health Service Commissioner's functions, and the provisions which apply to him and his investigations and reports, are on the same lines, with the necessary changes, as those which apply in the case of the

Commissioner for Local Administration (*q.v.*). The National Health Service (Scotland) Act 1972 should be consulted.

Hearsay evidence.—Hearsay evidence is primarily evidence of what a person, other than the person giving the evidence, has said. There are two kinds of hearsay, primary and secondary, secondary being the commoner and is dealt with here first.

Secondary hearsay is evidence given by one person of what he has been told by another about something which is in the direct knowledge of the other. The evidence should thus properly be given by the other and not by the one to whom he has passed the information. This is an application of the best evidence rule which requires that, if direct evidence is, or ought to be available it must be led. The general rule is thus that this kind of hearsay is not admissible as evidence. There are, however, exceptions to the rule. An example of secondary hearsay which may be admissible evidence is something which was said by a deceased person — that being the best evidence in the circumstances.

The question of primary evidence arises where it is necessary to prove that a statement has been made, *e.g.* in an action based on misrepresentation, damages for defamation or arising from a contract entered into orally or in a trial for perjury or extortion. The person leading such evidence is not concerned with the truth or otherwise of the statement. He may indeed maintain it is untrue, and it may be shown to be untrue by proving that the witness had previously made a different statement or that an extra-judicial admission or confession had been made. There are other instances on which primary hearsay may be admitted as evidence. It may, for instance, be used as proof of a person's state of mind or to explain the grounds on which a medical or other expert witness based his opinion.

Heritable property (also **Heritage**).—Heritable property includes all objects naturally immovable (such as land and minerals) or fixed to the soil such as buildings. Trees, annual crops (*e.g.* grain crops) and garden plants are heritable until cut and separated from the soil when they become moveable property. Rights connected with or affecting any heritable property (*e.g.* a lease of a farm, a **wayleave**) are also heritable. Rents of, or loans secured over, land are heritable though each payment when made is moveable. Similarly some continuing payments, *e.g.* a yearly premium or annuity, are heritable where succession to the creditor is in issue, though each payment when made and arrears of payments of an annuity are, moveable.

High Court of Justiciary.—This is the supreme criminal court of Scotland. It consists of the Lord Justice-General (who is the head of the court and the same person as the Lord President of the Court of Session), the **Lord Justice-Clerk** and the other judges of the Court of Session. When sitting in the Court of Justiciary judges are known as the Lords Commissioners of Justiciary and are clad in different robes from those which they wear when sitting in the Court of Session. The court sits in a number of towns as well as in Edinburgh. Scotland is divided into four circuits for this purpose, each circuit having its circuit towns.

The jurisdiction of the court extends over the whole of Scotland and covers all crimes which are not within the exclusive jurisdiction of other courts (*e.g.* offences which are to be tried in a court of summary jurisdiction). It has concurrent jurisdiction with the sheriff court over most crimes, but has exclusive jurisdiction over cases of treason, murder, rape, incest and some more technical crimes. All cases come before it on solemn procedure, as do some cases in the Sheriff Court also.

There is no appeal to the House of Lords, but there is an appeal on a question of law, in certain circumstances also on a question of fact, and against the sentence (both with leave of the court) to the **Court of Criminal Appeal.** As a trial court one only of the judges takes the case with a jury; as an appeal court three judges take the case without a jury. The appeal is from a decision of a trial court, or from a decision of a sheriff on indictment. Appeals from the district court are heard by the Court of Criminal Appeal also.

Hire Purchase.—See **Warranty.**

Holograph.—A deed or writing is holograph if the whole of it is written by the granter in his own hand. It is validly executed if signed at the end by the granter and it does not require to be witnessed. A holograph will is thus one written in the handwriting of the testator, and such a will usually states in the body or *in gremio* of the deed, that it is so written. A holograph deed of several pages does not need to be signed on each page.

A deed which is partly holograph, *e.g.* one partly printed or otherwise produced, and as to the remainder in the granter's handwriting and signed by him, is valid if the written parts and the essentials are sufficient by themselves to convey meaning and capable of receiving effect (if the signature of such a deed is authenticated by witnesses it is of course valid even if the holograph portions would not be capable of receiving effect by themselves).

A deed which is in no part holograph (*e.g.* typed) may be "adopted as holograph" if these words are written by the signatory preferably immediately above his signature. Some deeds, however, must have witnesses. (See **Attestation.**)

Homicide.—"Homicide is the destruction of a self-existent human life. It can be committed by any act or culpable omission resulting in death. It is divided into criminal and non-criminal homicide. Non-criminal homicide is either casual or justifiable. Casual homicide is by accident or mischance and is said to be restricted to cases in which the person accused of it was lawfully employed and not culpably careless; it is important only in relation to involuntary culpable homicide. Criminal homicide is divided into murder and culpable homicide. Culpable homicide can itself be divided into two crimes, firstly involuntary culpable homicide, which is distinguishable from murder by reference to *mens rea* [*q.v.*] involuntary culpable homicide being, roughly speaking, homicide which is neither intentional nor grossly reckless and secondly voluntary culpable homicide is murder under mitigating circumstances." The foregoing is an extract from *Criminal Law* by G. H. Gordon.

Homologation.—Homologation is a method by which a contract or agreement which has not been formally constituted can be given effect as if all formalities had been complied with. It is part of the general doctrine of **Personal bar** *videlicet* that a person cannot take up an attitude inconsistent with his own earlier words or conduct. Homologation is normally relied on to prevent a party backing out of a contract but it can be used in many circumstances where a person is attempting to avoid implementing an obligation which he is held to have approved. Homologation may be inferred from some act by the person against whom the contract or obligation is sought to be enforced which clearly shows that he has approved it. It cannot, of course be used to ratify a deed which is legally unenforceable.

A class of case in which the word homologation is (perhaps imprecisely) frequently used is that where an official of a corporation, company or other organisation takes some action, enters into some contract or agreement or undertakes some obligation ostensibly on behalf of, but not wholly within the scope of the authority delegated to him by, the organisation which then adopts and gives effect to its part of the act, contract, agreement or obligation as if it had been properly entered into in the first place.

Honorary sheriff.—Honorary sheriffs do not have to be legally qualified though many are. They are appointed by the sheriff principal of a sheriffdom to act as judges in the sheriffdom. They are not remunerated. They have the same jurisdiction as a sheriff and act when no sheriff is available or when there are a greater number of cases (usually minor criminal offence cases) to be dealt with than the sheriff is able to dispose of, or in other emergencies. They are in frequent session at weekends to deal with people who have been taken into police custody on say, a Friday evening, and who cannot be retained in custody or released without authority. They are also relied on to issue search warrants and other urgent authorities. There are over 400 honorary sheriffs throughout Scotland.

Hypothec.—Generally speaking, the only way in which security for debt can be obtained over corporeal moveable property is by the creditor taking possession of it. In certain limited circumstances, however, rights in security over moveables are recognised though the debtor continues to have possession of them. These are hypothecs and **liens**. Hypothecs are recognised legally or tacitly by settled custom in some cases and in others may be created by agreement or contract. A landlord has a right of hypothec in security of his claim for rent over his tenant's effects brought on to the premises let. It does not apply in respect of subjects let for agriculture and, in the case of lets regulated by the Houseletting and Rating Act 1911, bedding materials, goods and implements of trade used by the occupier or any member of his family as a means of livelihood are excepted. A solicitor may claim out of any expenses awarded to his client in a litigation sums advanced by him to the client by way of outlays and expenses of the litigation.

There are maritime liens, similar in effect to hypothecs, which enable a ship's master to recover his wages and disbursements on account of the ship and the crew have a similar right.

There are also conventional hypothecs. The owner or master of a ship may create a security over it without giving possession or making an entry in the ship's register and a bond granted by either may also create a security over the cargo.

Similar also are statutory hypothecs. See, for example, the Agricultural Credits (Scotland) Act 1929, the Companies (Floating Charges and Receivers) (Scotland) Act 1972, s. 31 of the Merchant Shipping Act 1894, and the schedule to the Mortgaging of Aircraft Order 1972 (S.I. 1972 No. 1268). (See also **Lien; Sequestration.**)

I

Illiquid.—This word occurs most frequently in the context of contracts involving payments of money. The amount due under such a contract is liquid after it has been finally ascertained and is thus of a fixed amount. Before that has happened, the amount due by the debtor is illiquid.

Improvement notice.—This is a notice given by an inspector appointed under s. 19 of the Health and Safety at Work, etc. Act 1974 by the Health and Safety Executive or by any other authority which is responsible for the enforcement of the provisions of (1) Part 1 of the Act; or (2) any regulation made under s. 15 of that Act or (3) regulations made under s. 30 of the Agriculture (Safety, Health and Welfare Provisions) Act 1956; or (4) any provisions in or regulations made under any of the Acts mentioned in Schedule 1 to the 1974 Act. The notice is served on any person in whose case the inspector is of opinion that he is contravening one or other of the above provisions or regulations or has contravened any such provision and the contravention will be repeated. The inspector must specify the provisions in question, give particulars of the reasons for his opinion and require that the contravention should be remedied within the period specified in the notice. There are provisions in regulations enabling the person on whom the notice is served to appeal against it and for an extension of the period specified in the notice.

Inadmissible evidence.—See **Admissible evidence.**

In camera.—Camera is the judge's room behind the court. When a matter comes before the judge in camera he deals with it in his room. Certain matters must be dealt with in camera such as a petition presented by a procurator fiscal to the sheriff in a case in which the crime alleged to have been committed might lead to a trial by solemn procedure.

Incapax.—The Latin word *incapax* means, as nearly as may be in English, "not capable". It is used not only as an adjective but also loosely as a noun. A person who is incapable, because of mental or other ill-health, of dealing with his own affairs or of giving instructions for their management, is *incapax* and he is himself referred to as an *incapax*. A person who is rendered unfit by reason of injuries sustained *e.g.* in an accident or who suffers some physical incapacity is, except in special circumstances such as blindness or paralysis or severe injury, not under legal incapacity. For the management of the affairs of an *incapax* a *curator bonis* is appointed by the court and the curator transacts all the business of the *incapax* including the raising or defending of actions in court. During a lucid interval a person who was *incapax* may be capable of dealing with his affairs and can then, for example, make a valid will but while insane may not be capable even of wrongdoing. Drunkenness may render a person temporarily incapable of transacting business, and such business as he does transact during a period of drunkenness may be **voidable.**

Incorporation.—The Companies Acts 1948-1980 make general provision for the incorporation of a company by registration by the Registrar of Companies of the company's memorandum and articles of association containing its constitution and objects and the regulations for its management. Fees and stamp duties are payable and a certificate of incorporation is issued by the Registrar, the company thus coming into existence as a legal entity. The certificate is conclusive that all formalities have been complied with and that the company is registered. The Registrar of Companies, who maintains a list of all Scottish and English companies and business names, has an office in Edinburgh.

Incorporeal moveable property.—Incorporeal moveable property is not tangible. It has no body or substance. It comes into existence in various ways. Some instances are decrees of court for payment of sums of money, a claim for debt arising because a sum due under contract has not been paid, a right of action for damages arising from a breach of obligation (*e.g.* where the driver of a vehicle causes damage to another as a result of negligent driving). **Negotiable instruments** (*q.v.*) are a special class of incorporeal moveable rights and documents of title to goods such as delivery orders.

Indemnity.—Indemnities are similar to cautionary obligations (see **Caution**). They may be defined as being undertakings given by one person to protect another from damage or loss or to make on behalf of the other a payment to a third party which the other owes to that party. An example is where a contractor undertakes to indemnify his employer against claims by third parties arising out of his operations under the contract. Whether the right to indemnification arises in any circumstances rests on an interpretation of the words used.

Indenture.—An indenture is a deed made by more parties than one. It is so called because there ought to be as many copies as there are parties and formerly each copy was cut or indented like the teeth of a saw or by a wavy line to correspond with the others. Its use in Scots law (without indentation) is now almost wholly confined to the title of the deed by which one party, the master (*e.g.* a solicitor), enters into an agreement with another, the pupil, to instruct, teach and generally prepare the other to practise or perform work in the master's profession. No person can qualify, *e.g.* as a solicitor, without serving an apprenticeship under indenture.

Indictable offence.—Offences are, generally speaking, criminal acts less serious than crimes, but there is no clear-cut distinction between the two. The word "offence" is, however, usually employed to denote something that is prohibited by statute. But it is difficult to generalise. A statutory offence such as a breach of

49

parking regulations is far removed from the concept of a crime, but an offence such as a bad case of drunken, dangerous or reckless driving is very much nearer to that concept. Because a statutory offence may or may not be serious according to the circumstances it is quite usual to provide that it may be prosecuted either summarily or on indictment and it will then be for the prosecution to elect whether the one or the other is proper in the particular case, remembering that a conviction on indictment always carries heavier penalties than a summary conviction. An indictable offence is in the latter class. (See **Indictment**).

Indictment.—All prosecutions before the High Court of Justiciary or before the sheriff sitting with a jury proceed on indictment in name of the the Lord Advocate. An indictment must be in, or as nearly as may be in, one of the forms set out in Schedule A to the Criminal Procedure (Scotland) Act 1887 and must be signed by the Lord Advocate or one of his deputes or by a procurator fiscal (the words "By Authority of Her Majesty's Advocate" appearing before the fiscal's signature). The indictment is served on the accused and charges him with the commission of a serious offence or crime. Whether or not the crime is serious enough to warrant the accused being charged on indictment is decided by the Lord Advocate or may be prescribed by statute. The procedure on a prosecution on indictment is called solemn procedure as opposed to summary procedure followed in less serious cases. Section 8 of the Criminal Justice (Scotland) Act 1980 provides that certain summary offences may be tried on indictment.

Induciae.—A Latin tag which connotes the period within which a person must take action in connection with a matter of which he has been given legal notice. It is most frequently used in the context of court proceedings and refers for instance to the period of time within which the defender in a civil action must intimate to the court his intention to defend the action.

Infeftment.—The symbolic act (now obsolete) of putting an heir into possession of heritable property and so completing his title. In the case of house property in a burgh the act was the handing by the owner of the property to the heir of a hasp and staple — the clasp and hoop to which a padlock was attached for fastening a door.

In flagrante delicto.—Describes the position of a person who is discovered or apprehended in the act of committing a crime.

In gremio.—See **Holograph.**

Inhibition.—Inhibition has been defined as "a personal prohibition prohibiting the party inhibited from burdening, alienating directly or indirectly or otherwise affecting his lands or other heritable property to the prejudice of the creditor inhibiting". The creditor may proceed to inhibit his debtor if granted warrant to do so by the Court of Session on an application made to the court by him. The inhibition is effective when it is registered in the Register of Inhibitions and Adjudications kept by the Keeper of the Registers. Burdening includes for example the granting of a bond (mortgage) over land or buildings in security of sums borrowed and alienating includes for example selling the land or building. Inhibition may also be used by a husband to terminate his wife's presumed authority (known as "the wife's *praepositura*") to act as agent in all matters of household administration, *e.g.* to purchase goods such as food and household necessities or to engage tradesmen to do repairs to household gas, electricity, sewage or water systems. Letters of inhibition against her are deemed to be made known to all when recorded in the Register of Inhibitions and Adjudications. (See **Diligence.**)

In hoc statu.—Used to make clear that a problem or dispute is being considered in light of the facts as they exist at the time or "at this stage".

Initial writ.—The initial writ is the document by which an ordinary action in the sheriff court is begun. But for its name its various parts are the same as those of a summons by which an action in the Court of Session is begun.

In limine.—Literally "on the threshold". A proposition made at the outset of an action.

Inner House.—See **Court of Session.**

Inter alia.—This Latin phrase has no specifically legal meaning but is much used by lawyers. A simple meaning is "among other things". There are related phrases, such as *inter alios* (among other persons); *inter se* (between ourselves) and *inter vivos* (between living persons), as in **Donation inter vivos** (*q.v.*).

Interdict.—Interdict is a remedy effected by decree of court, to prevent wrong, harm or injury being done to a person (or which that person anticipates may be done to him) or to property belonging to him. It proceeds on the basis that prevention is better than cure. The conduct on which the complaint is based must amount to some appreciable wrong, harm or injury (not necessarily physical injury). Reasonable grounds for fearing such conduct is sufficient. If the court grants interdict it must state precisely what acts it is designed to prevent. But it cannot require the defender to take any specific course of action or to do any specific thing, except make good any harm or injury already done. Interdict is an equitable remedy which will be granted if the court is satisfied that it is appropriate in the case.

Interdict may be granted *ad interim* (for the time being) to preserve affairs in their existing state pending a decision of the court. The remedy is not available if some statutory remedy which would achieve the desired end is available. (See **Declarator; Ex parte.**)

Interlocutor.—An interlocutor is strictly an order or decision of a court which does not finally dispose of the case but is given in the course of the proceedings. In practice it applies to any order of the court.

Intestate.—If a person dies without having made a valid will or other testamentary writing disposing of the property which he or she owns or is in a position to dispose of at the time of his or her death, he or she is said to have died intestate and he or she can be referred to as "the intestate". The intestate's means and estate are then disposed of according to the rules of intestate succession. It is also possible for a person to die partially intestate. In such a case he or she will have left a **testamentary**

writing which does not, or does not properly, dispose of the whole of his estate.

Intromissions.—See **Account of charge and discharge.**

Ipso facto.—By the very act or fact; an expression frequently used to make clear that an act or proceeding which is prohibited is not to have even *prima facie* validity — it is *ipso facto* null and void.

Ipso jure.—By virtue of law — frequently used to make clear that an act or proceeding is, by law, null and void.

In re.—These words are widely used in England in court procedure to mean "in the matter of" an action by, say, A against B. In Scotland they mean simply "in regard to". For instance, *in re mercatoria* means in regard to matters arising out of trade or of a transaction in which a matter of trade is in issue.

Inter se.—Between two or more people.

Inter vivos.—Between living persons (see **Donation inter vivos**).

Irregular marriage.—Before the Marriage (Scotland) Act 1939 became law in July 1940 there were three modes in which what has been called "an irregular marriage" could be entered into. The procedures were derived from the canon law and from a Scottish statute of the sixteenth century.

The first of the three was marriage by declaration by the parties in the presence of witnesses of consent to take each other as man and wife. Writing was not essential. The conduct of the parties as spouses might suffice.

The second method was marriage by promise in words by the parties that they would become man and wife and that they subsequently had sexual intercourse in reliance of the promise. Marriages which took place in either of these ways *before* 1 July 1940 have remained good thereafter.

The third method is marriage by cohabitation with habit and repute. An Act of the Scottish Parliament in 1503 provided that a woman who had been reputed to be a man's wife during his lifetime should be entitled to the legal right of "terce" (which no longer exists) out of his estate after his death. From this arose the doctrine that if a couple cohabit openly and constantly as husband and wife so as to produce a general belief that they are married they will be presumed to have exchanged matrimonial consent. This mode of irregular marriage remains competent.

That a marriage has been constituted by habit and repute can be conclusively established only by decree of the Court of Session on application made to it by one of the parties.

There are now two methods of contracting a regular marriage, namely before a minister of religion or before an authorised registrar of deaths, births and marriages.

Irrelevant.—The general meaning of this word is "not bearing upon, or applying to, the matter in hand; not pertinent." When used in a legal context it has a similar meaning. (See **Admissible evidence** for a legal context in which it is important.)

Ish, the.—See **Lease.**

Issue.—This word has a number of meanings. In law it has two particular meanings which are important. The first is, formally, the fruit of the body, that is children (excluding stepchildren) and, it

52

may be, adopted children. The second is one way of describing a matter either legal or factual which is in dispute before a court or other tribunal.

J

Joint and several liability.—Where two or more persons are taken bound by contract to perform some work or to make payment of a sum of money, the general rule is that each is bound to perform or make payment of his share only and not to make payment of or perform the whole. They are, to put it another way, bound *pro rata* for payment of the sum due. But there are exceptional cases in which the debtors under the contract are bound jointly as well as severally (that is separately as individuals). In such cases the creditor may recover the whole debt from any one or more of the debtors. The commonest of these exceptional cases is that in which the contract itself binds the debtors jointly and severally.

Joint tenancy.—A joint tenancy exists where two or more persons become the lessees of land, buildings, minerals, fishings, or any other subjects which can be leased. The joint tenants hold the subjects as lessees for the period agreed on or specified in the lease. Each is tenant of the whole of the subjects and they are jointly and severally (individually) liable for payment of the rent and for compliance with the other conditions of the lease. If one of the joint tenants dies his interest in the lease accrues to the survivors, unless provision to the contrary is made in the lease. Each is entitled to possession of the subjects let, each has his own interest and title.

Judicial examination.—When a person is brought before the sheriff or a district court to be charged with a crime a judicial examination takes place. This has been of little importance in Scotland since 1908 when it was made unnecessary for an accused person to make any declaration at this stage of the proceedings in answer to the charge and normally no answer is in fact made. The examination is therefore purely formal and the accused makes his statement in defence (or otherwise) at a later stage. This procedure has recently been altered by s. 6 of the Criminal Justice (Scotland) Act 1980.

Another use of the expression occurs where a person has been found by the sheriff to be bankrupt. A day is fixed by the sheriff for the public examination (judicial examination) of the bankrupt and his whole affairs including assets and liabilities.

Judicial factor.—A judicial factor is a person, usually an accountant or solicitor, appointed by the Court of Session or the sheriff court to manage and administer the property and affairs of another. The usual reason for the appointment is to avoid danger of loss (*e.g.* where the owner is **incapax**) or to resolve a deadlock in administration (*e.g.* where assets are lying in a deceased person's estate and there is no executor or trustee, or there is disagreement between executors or trustees or between them and beneficiaries). A petition must be made to the court for the appointment of a factor, and he acts as an officer of the court, his powers and duties being for the most part laid down in **statute** (*q.v.*) and **Acts of Sederunt.** He is subject to the supervision of the **Accountant of Court,** who audits his accounts annually. Any failure of duty by the factor is reported by the Accountant to the court who may, if the circumstances demand, remove the factor from office. But see Judicial Factors Act 1849 as amended most recently in ss. 7 and 14 of the Law Reform (Miscellaneous Provisions) (Scotland) Act 1980.

Judicial redress.—This expression simply means what it says. The courts redress (set right) wrongs done to members of the community. The expression is used to distinguish between the redress which the courts provide and the redress which a person obtains, for what good it may do him, outwith the law (perhaps by using his fists) to repay injury with injury. Such a person has, colloquially speaking, taken the law into his own hands.

Jurisdiction.—This word has several meanings. Its most common use is in relation to the area within which a court has power to entertain (try or hear) cases. The Court of Session has jurisdiction throughout Scotland; a sheriff court has jurisdiction in the sheriff court district. A second meaning relates to the actions which a particular court has power to deal with. The Court of Session has for instance exclusive jurisdiction in divorce actions, the sheriff court has no jurisdiction in such actions but has exclusive jurisdiction in actions for sums of money or damages of £500 or less. A third meaning arises from the fact that a court does not have jurisdiction over all persons who are in the court's area at any particular time and that there are means by which the court may acquire jurisdiction over a person over whom it would not otherwise have jurisdiction. For instance, the possession of moveable property in Scotland does not confer jurisdiction on the Scottish courts to try actions against the possessor unless the property is arrested.

Juror.—A juror is, strictly, a member of a jury convened for the purpose of hearing a trial although any person on the list of potential jurymen kept by the sheriff clerk may be, rather inaccurately, referred to as a juror. There are rules about those members of the public who are entitled to be jurors and those who are exempt from, or are not permitted to undertake, jury service, and there are rules also about the composition of juries. Where a jury is to be convened to hear a trial in the High Court when it is on circuit, the sheriff clerk of the sheriffdom in which the trial is to take place sends a notice to persons (in number exceeding those required to form a jury) citing them to be at court on the date of the trial. Where the jury is to deal with a civil case in the Court of Session, the sheriff clerk of Lothian and Borders cites the jurors. The selection of those to serve on the jury takes place in court, the names of those cited and present being read out by the sheriff clerk and objections to any of them being stated by the lawyers representing the pursuer and the defender in a civil case, by the prosecutor and the accused or his lawyer in a criminal case. Similar procedure is followed where the trial is in the sheriff court but, s. 11 of the Law Reform (Miscellaneous Provisions) (Scotland) Act 1980 abolished jury trials in civil actions in the sheriff court and ss. 1-3 and later sections of the same Act made changes in the law about jurors. Where a trial is to take place in the High Court of Justiciary in Edinburgh the Clerk of Justiciary sends notices to persons who may be called as jurors in the particular case.

Jus quaesitum tertio.—This Latin maxim gives expression to a rule of much importance in the law of contract. In the ordinary case where a contract is made between two parties it is they alone who acquire rights under and have liabilities imposed on them by it. One of the most important exceptions to this rule is that, where it appears that the object of the contract was to benefit a third party, the contract may be held to confer a *jus quaesitum tertio* on that person. Such a right will be held to have been conferred if the third party is named, or referred to, or is one of a distinct identifiable class referred to, in the contract. Instances in which such a right exists are where money is placed on **deposit receipt** (*q.v.*) made payable to the third party or where building restrictions are imposed on co-tenants (or co-feuars) and there is a reference in the title deeds to a common feuing plan or a stipulation in the title of each co-tenant that the same restrictions are to be imposed on all the co-tenants. In the first case the third party can uplift the sum on deposit; in the second any one of the co-tenants (or co-feuars) can raise an action in court to enforce the restrictions on any other in breach of any of them.

Jus relictae and **Jus relicti.**—See **Legal rights.**

Justice of the Peace.—Part II of the District Courts (Scotland) Act 1975 contains detailed provisions about the appointment and removal from office of justices of the peace, about persons who are disqualified from being appointed as justices, and about instruction of them to fit them for the performance of their duties. The names of justices who are over 70 years of age are for that or for a number of other reasons entered in the Supplementary list of Justices. Justices in Scotland are appointed on behalf and in name of the Sovereign by instrument under the hand of the Secretary of State for Scotland. Each is appointed for a particular commission area, and a record of all those holding the office is kept. Justices are the "judges" in a district court, and have a number of other functions, *e.g.* they can certify the identity and photographs of applicants for passports.

L

Lammas.—Lammas is the first day of August (the feast of first fruits) and is a quarter day in Scotland formerly, and still to some extent, of importance in the context of the change of tenancy or ownership of agricultural land.

Lands Tribunal for Scotland.—The function of this tribunal (referred to elsewhere herein) is to settle disputes about compensation for acquisition of land, to vary or discharge conditions etc., with which land is burdened, to allocate a feuduty which burdens more than one area of land between the several areas. An appeal by way of stated case against a decision of the tribunal may be made to the Court of Session and thence to the House of Lords. Decisions of the tribunal are reported in the *Scots Law Times*.

Law agent.—A common term (often shortened to "agent") for a solicitor. The expression was given significance by a number of statutes (*e.g.* the Law Agents Act 1873) but is not much employed now, either in a statutory context or in day-to-day usage. "Solicitor" is almost invariably used in modern statutes and in connection, for instance, with the Law Society of Scotland.

Lawburrows.—The word burrow (the same in derivation as borgh) anciently meant a cautioner (see **Caution**), and the action of "law-burrows" was one in which a person who had, or believed he had, reason to fear danger from another could, if he satisfied the court that his fear was well-grounded, move the court to order the other to find caution not to molest him. If the court made such an order but the defender failed to find caution a penalty of imprisonment for not more than six months could be imposed. Further, if there was a failure to comply with the order the amount of the caution could be recovered in a civil action by the pursuer. Though still competent the action is now seldom used for that purpose. It is more commonly used by a woman afraid for her safety in domestic disputes.

Lawyer.—This is a generic term which covers all persons who are part of or are connected with the legal profession and are qualified to and practise in the law. It includes solicitors, advocates and judges of the Court of Session and the sheriff court.

Lease.—A lease (infrequently, in modern times, called a "tack") is the letting on hire of lands, buildings or other **heritable subjects** (*q.v.*) for a specific period on conditions including payment by the tenant to the landlord (usually the owner of the subjects let) of a rent. The return may not be a money payment, it may be in goods. The law as it applies to leases is a very wide subject and difficult not only to understand but to ascertain. There is an immense volume of legislation superimposed on common law. The law relating to letting of dwelling houses differs substantially from that relating to the letting of agricultural holdings (farms, smallholdings, crofts); to the lettings of minerals, fishings and shootings; to furnished houses; to houses let by an employer to his employee and to other kinds of subjects. A lease is a contract; there must be a period specified for its duration; if the period is for longer than a year it must, to be binding on the parties, be in writing; the amount of the rent payable must be specified, as must also the date at which the lease is to be terminated (the legal term for which is the "ish").

Legacy.—In general, the word legacy means anything, usually moveable (*e.g.* money, articles of value), bequeathed to a person by will.

Legal aid.—This matter cannot be dealt with at any length here. Aid is available to a person in a civil court action (whether the pursuer or the defender in the action) who has not got means

56

of an amount laid down by rules made under the Legal Aid and Advice (Scotland) Acts 1967 and 1972. The aid available varies with the means of the applicant. There is an elaborate procedure for determining availability; it is carried out by the Law Society of Scotland, who are required to set up local committees and a central committee to deal with these matters. In a criminal case legal aid is available to the accused person, the amount, if any, of the aid being determined by the court dealing with the case.

Legal person.—A legal person is an individual or entity who or which has legal rights and on whom or which legal duties are imposed. The category is not confined to natural living persons but extends also, at least for some purpose, to certain associations of living persons (for example partnerships). It also includes for all purposes certain entities, groups or institutions held to be incorporated by law, for example companies to which the Companies Acts 1948 to 1980 apply and local authorities. They exist in law quite independently of the legal persons who govern, or are employed by, them. Whether the **Crown** is or is not a corporation is uncertain.

Legal rights.—These are rights which persons who survive certain of their close relatives are entitled to claim out of the deceaseds' estates. The rights of any such person are not destroyed by the rights of other relatives entitled to succeed to the deceased's estate on intestacy and, with some qualifications, are not interfered with by the deceased's will if he or she leaves one. They do not, however, take precedence over **prior rights** payable out of the estate. The subject cannot be dealt with here in any detail. The following sets out the rights which now exist in the estate of a person who died after 10 September 1964 when the Succession (Scotland) Act 1964 came into operation and of the persons entitled to them. They are:

(1) The right of a widow to a share of her deceased husband's moveable estate (see **Moveables**) known technically as *jus relictae*. The right is based on common law and is to one-third of the estate if children of his and the widow's or of a former marriage of his, or of issue of predeceasing children, also survive. If there are no children, or if all the children have renounced their claims to a share of the estate, the widow takes one-half. The claim is against the net moveable estate after deduction of the deceased's debts, deathbed and funeral expenses and the expenses of winding up the estate. It is in the nature of a debt and, as has been said above, is payable after a surviving spouse's claim, if any, to prior rights has been met. The estate is that ascertained as at the date of death.

(2) The right of a widower to share in his deceased wife's estate, known technically as *jus relicti*. The right is the same as the widow's right to *jus relictae* dealt with in (1) above. The right is a statutory one (see the Married Women's Property (Scotland) Act 1881). The Conjugal Rights (Scotland) Act 1861 provides that, if the wife divorces the husband, he has no claim for *jus relicti*.

(3) The right of a child (including an illegitimate child) and of grandchildren or remoter descendants (where a child has predeceased), to a share in a deceased parent's (or grandparent's) moveable estate. This right is known as "legitim"

or "bairn's part". It is payable out of the estate of each parent, and is not affected if the father predeceases the mother or the mother the father. The claim is to one-third of the net moveable estate (see (1) above) if there is also a surviving **spouse** (*q.v.*) or if the surviving spouse has renounced his or her legal rights. The claim is a debt due to any child entitled to legitim.

The rules about the computation of the estate out of which legitim is paid are substantially the same as at (1) above. All children of the deceased, no matter who the father or, as the case may be, the mother be, are entitled to legitim but the grandchildren or remoter descendants are entitled between them only to the share to which their parent, if he predeceased, would have been entitled if he had survived. The children are entitled to share equally in the legitim fund. Sums paid by a parent during his or her lifetime to a child are deemed to be advances of legitim and, so as to maintain equality between children claiming legitim, any such advances must be added to the fund out of which the legitim is to be paid and are then set against the share of the whole fund falling to that child. A parent can never deprive any person of his or her title to legitim nor apportion the legitim fund otherwise than in accordance with the rules of law. If the deceased leaves a will and any child is a beneficiary under it, he has the right to elect to take under the will or to claim legitim but not to do both. An adopted child has the same right to legitim as a natural child but a stepchild has no claim.

Legislation.—Legislation is all the provisions enacted by Parliament (the Scots Parliament before 1707, the Parliament of Great Britain from 1707 to 1800, the United Kingdom Parliament since 1800) and by EEC Regulations and Directives since 1972 (*q.v.*).

Legitim.—See **Legal rights.**

Lesion enorm (more commonly **Enorm Lesion**).—The ordinary meaning of the word lesion is hurt or injury; Scots law adds detriment and loss. Enorm means considerable. The words used together are of importance in relation to contracts entered into by minors. Where a minor in entering into a contract undertakes to give or do something for much less than he should have got, he is said to have suffered enorm lesion. It must be positive loss, not loss of possible gain. Such a contract can be reduced by the court on the application of the minor at any time before the expiry of the **quadriennium utile** (*q.v.*). Enorm lesion is presumed in the case of gifts, a surrender of rights, cautionary obligations, loans of money to the minor and in certain other circumstances. (See **Reduction.**)

Liable relative.—This expression is used in the context of social security. If, for instance, supplementary benefit is paid to meet the requirements of a **spouse** (*q.v.*) or a child which the husband or father or other relative is liable to meet, the Supplementary Benefits officers may if the spouse or child does not take action, themselves take action to recover the cost from the person liable.

Lien.—This is dealt with under the title **Hypothec** above. In addition to what is said there, a lien exists over goods entrusted for repair or for carriage, or title deeds, business books, the clothes of a guest at an hotel, but not over money deposited for a specific purpose only. It is an equitable right controlled by the court, who exceptionally may refuse to give it effect. A solicitor's right of lien is good against everyone (it is preferred to anyone else's claim on his client's estate), but, in other cases, it is good only against the claims of creditors.

Liferent.—There are two varieties of liferent, proper and improper. A proper liferent is a right to possess, use and enjoy heritable subjects during the grantee's lifetime without destroying or wasting their substance, and only a fiar and liferenter are involved. An improper liferent may be a right to enjoy moveable subjects on a mixed estate of heritable and moveable subjects, and where trustees are interposed between the liferenter and the fiar.

Limitations of actions.—There is a large number of limits imposed by various statutes on the time within which actions to establish rights for certain purposes may be raised in court. In legal theory the remedy provided is the cutting off of the right of action at the end of the period of limitation, whereas if the negative **prescription** (*q.v.*), which is similar in intention, operates, the right (not the right of action) is extinguished. However, for practical purposes the effect is similar. Not all of the limitations can be mentioned here. One of the most important is that a claim for personal injuries or death as the result of an act, neglect or default (see **Solatium** where this point is dealt with in part) must be brought within three years from the date when the injuries were sustained or of the date when the act, neglect or default ceased or from the date of death (see ss. 17-19 of the Prescription and Limitation (Scotland) Act 1973).

Other limitations on the time within which an action may be raised will be met with in many statutes.

Periods of limitation may be extended in some cases beyond the time specified in particular statutes. Examples are limitations relating to collisions at sea and social security benefits. It should be noted that, if an action is not begun within the period specified in the particular statute, the injured person or those entitled to damages in respect of a person's death have no remedy (see s. 23 of the Law Reform (Miscellaneous Provisions) (Scotland) Act 1980).

Liquidate damages.—Liquidate damages is a sum of money for payment of which in the event of a breach of contract provision is made in the contract. The payment is to be made by the party in breach and there may be difficulty in determining whether the payment is for liquidate damages or is a penalty. The essence of liquidate damages is that the sum stipulated for in the contract is a genuine pre-estimate of damage and not simply an attempt to ensure compliance with the contract by imposing a penalty. The question whether it is the one or the other is a matter of construction, to be decided on the terms and circumstances of the particular contract.

Liquidator.—Liquidation is the procedure of dissolving or "winding-up" bankrupt companies. Liquidation may be ordered by the Court of Session or, where the paid-up capital of the company does not exceed £10,000, by the sheriff court. If

59

ordered by the court it is called "judicial liquidation"; if decided on by the shareholders it is voluntary. But the voluntary liquidation may be supervised by the court. The liquidation is carried out by a liquidator and where the court orders or supervises a liquidation it also appoints one or more liquidators who thereby become officers of the court and subject to its jurisdiction. If the liquidation is voluntary the liquidator is appointed at a general meeting of the company. The function of the liquidator, put in general terms, is to ingather assets, adjust the rights of creditors and settle their claims so far as the assets permit. If there are surplus assets the liquidator distributes the surplus amongst the shareholders. The liquidator is not a trustee and is not vested in the assets of the company. He is an administrator whose duty is to ensure that the creditors' interests are protected. The Companies Act 1948 (ss. 237 to 245, except 239) contains provisions about the liquidator's appointment, the security he has to provide, his powers and other matters connected with the performance of his duties.

Locum tenens.—This term is applied to a person who acts as a deputy or substitute for some other person, *e.g.* a doctor or clergyman who is absent from his charge while on holiday or other necessary occasion.

Locus poenitentia.—These words refer to the opportunity made available to a person to withdraw from a contract which is not binding on account of its informality *e.g.* where it should be, but is not, in writing and has not been legally confirmed by the actings of the parties. Where the actings would render it inequitable to hold that the contract should be withdrawn from, they may be held to amount to **rei interventus.**

Lord Advocate.—The Lord Advocate is the senior of the two law officers of the Crown in Scotland (the other is the **Solicitor-General for Scotland** (*q.v.*)). He is selected by the Prime Minister, must be an experienced advocate (usually a Member of Parliament). He is responsible in the last resort for advising the government and its ministers who have functions in Scotland on all matters of law with which they are concerned, and he may be called as defender in any civil action against any government department or agency. He may himself, and sometimes does, appear in court on behalf of some government department, particularly where the action is one in which a declarator of the law is being sought in connection with some administrative action of the department. The Lord Advocate is also responsible for the taking of all criminal proceedings in Scotland (except in a few instances), but in the case of civil matters he relies largely on the Solicitor-General and in criminal cases on the advocates-depute, the Crown Office officials and the procurators fiscal (see under the headings dealing with each of these categories).

The Lord Advocate is also the minister of his own department (the Lord Advocate's Department) which is located in London. All Parliamentary Bills applying to Scotland are drafted there and those applying to Great Britain are adapted to take account of Scots law. Additionally he has ministerial functions in connection with the jurisdiction and procedure of the civil courts and certain tribunals, enforcement of foreign judgments and proposals for reform of the law proposed by the Scottish Law Commission. The Scottish Courts Administration carry out these functions on his behalf. In more recent times, where the Lord Advocate has not been a Member of Parliament, he has been made a life peer and deals with Scots legal matters in the House of Lords. Like any other minister, he demits office when the government of which he is a member resigns.

Lord Advocate's Department.—See **Lord Advocate.**

Lord Justice-Clerk.—The Lord Justice-Clerk ranks second after the **Lord President** in judicial status in the Court of Session. The office is as old as that of the Lord President and the holder of it is the senior and presiding judge in the Second Division of the Inner House of the court, and has the same functions in that Division as the Lord President has in the First Division. He deputises for the Lord President as occasion demands as head of the court and shares with the latter the duties associated with the administration of the court and disposal of its business. He is appointed by the Crown.

Lord Justice-General.—The Lord Justice-General is the Head of the **High Court of Justiciary,** and since 1830 when the office was merged with that of **Lord President** has been held by the same person as holds office as Lord President. Indeed, it may be mentioned under this title, all the judges of the Court of Session are also judges of the Court of Justiciary. The High Court of Justiciary is both a trial court and appeal court. When it sits as the Court of Criminal Appeal it consists of three judges, the Lord Justice-General being the presiding judge if he is available. The origin of the office is obscure and first appears in an Act of 1487 of the Scots Parliament. In earlier times, members of the nobility who had no legal qualifications were frequently appointed to it.

Lord Lyon.—The Lord Lyon King of Arms is both principal administrative officer and judge (having the same status as a Lord Ordinary) in Scottish heraldic matters. He also has administrative duties such as the granting of armorial bearings, the delivery of Royal Proclamations and conduct of state ceremonials. The Lyon Court now consists of the Lyon sitting alone but an appeal may be made from a decision of his to the Court of Session and thence to the House of Lords.

Lord Ordinary.—All the judges of the Court of Session other than the Lords President and Justice-Clerk and the other six judges who are members of the First and Second Divisions are referred to as "Lords Ordinary", and comprise the Outer House of the court. Any judge who sits in either Division may also sit as a Lord Ordinary in the Outer House when the need arises. The Lords Ordinary are the judges of first instance in the Court of Session, that is, they deal with all cases which are initiated in the Court of Session and their decisions are subject to appeal to the Inner House (the Divisions deal also with appeals from other sources). The Lords Ordinary are not Lords of Appeal and thus cases such as special and stated cases which come by way of appeal to the court are not heard by them, though some have special functions for the performance of which they are appointed by the Lord President. An example of the last is the Lord Ordinary on Exchequer Causes.

Lord President.—The Lord President is the head of the whole Court of Session which currently consists of 21 judges (referred to as "the Senators of the College of Justice" or "the Lords of Council and Session"). The office is very ancient but was given statutory existence by the Act of the Scots Parliament of 1532 which founded the court. The duties of the office have been added to and altered over the centuries. He is the presiding judge of the First Division of the Inner House of the court and takes charge of its proceedings. As head of the court he takes responsibility for the preparation of all **Acts of Sederunt** (*q.v.*) and it is his signature which authenticates that any such Act has been made. He also has responsibility in general for the administration of the court as a whole and for the disposal of its business. Amongst his other functions are the nomination of persons for appointment to a number of offices including chairmen of industrial and other tribunals, and he is consulted (in some instances as required by statute) by the Secretary of State, the Lord Advocate and other ministers in connection with other appointments. Many duties similar to his are performed in England by the Lord Chancellor.

M

Majority.—The term is descriptive of the status of a person who has attained adulthood and therefore full legal capacity both as to rights and liabilities as a member of society. The age at which majority in this sense is attained is now 18 years — the 18th anniversary of the date of the person's birth. Before 1970 the age was 21 years. The word also has the more general meaning of the greater number. Thus to say, for instance, that a motion was carried by a "majority" means that a greater number voted for than against it.

Maladministration.—In general terms maladministration is bad management, especially of public affairs. The word has no specific legal significance, but where a person who holds any office performs the functions of the office in such a manner as to cause, unjustifiably, loss to those to whom he owes a duty to perform them properly, the person suffering loss may have a right to raise an action for damages against him. In more recent times the word has come to be applied more commonly to the unsatisfactory actings, sometimes amounting to injustice of, for instance, government departments, local authorities, hospital authorities or their officials or members of staff. If no legal remedy is available the **Ombudsman** (*q.v.*) may be approached.

Malice.—The motive underlying conduct may be good or bad or it may be malicious, but generally speaking a good motive does not clear a person of the charge of a fault or crime, nor does a bad motive prove him to have been at fault or to have committed a crime. Malice in the sense of intention to injure is synonymous with intentional or deliberate wrongdoing. Malice in the sense of hatred, spite, malevolence or ill-will is relevant only exceptionally in those cases where a malicious motive is relevant, *e.g.*

defamation, malicious falsehood or wrongful use of **diligence** (*q.v.*). It is also any indirect or improper motive other than a sense of duty. Whether any of these exist is a question of law to be decided by the court in course of the action in which they arise.

Mandate.—A mandate is a contract by which one person empowers another to act on his behalf in general or in some special respect. The person to whom the mandate is given (called the "mandatory") acts gratuitously and thus all commissions for the transaction of business where no fee is contracted for are proper mandates. Where granted in writing, the mandate may take the form of a factory and commission or **Power of attorney** (*q.v.*) or, where the granter is to be represented at a meeting, a **proxy.** A mandatory cannot engage some other person to carry out the work he has undertaken to perform and he must not do anything outwith the terms of the mandate (see **Ultra vires**). If he does either he may be liable in damages to the party with whom he deals.

Mandatory.—See **Mandate.**

Marriage.—This is the ceremony or process by which the legal relationship of husband and wife is constituted. There are two modes of contracting a regular marriage and one of contracting an irregular marriage. The relationship or contract between a husband and wife is referred to specifically or impliedly in many contexts throughout this book. See, *e.g.* **Irregular marriage, Dissolution of marriage, Divorce, Void, Voidable, Legal** and **Prior rights.** See also Marriage (Scotland) Act 1956 and Marriage (Scotland) Act 1977 as amended by s. 21 of the Law Reform (Miscellaneous Provisions) (Scotland) Act 1980.

Martinmas.—Martinmas (the mass or feast of St Martin) is a term day in Scotland which falls on 11 November. But s. 4 of the Removal Terms (Scotland) Act 1886 provides that, in the absence of express provision to the contrary, a tenant whose term of entry is Martinmas will enter or remove from the premises leased to him on 28 November (or on the following day if the 28 is a Sunday).

Memorial.—This word has a special legal meaning. If the opinion of a person particularly well versed in the law or a particular aspects of it is desired on some point which has arisen, the opinion is sought by a solicitor who prepares a written document (referred to as a "memorial") in which the facts out of which the question has arisen are narrated and the question itself is asked. The opinion of senior rather than junior counsel (see **Counsel**) is most frequently sought but in certain fields, conveyancing for instance, the opinion of a person who is a professor in the particular field may be sought.

Mens rea.—This Latin tag means a guilty or criminal intent or state of mind. The general rule is that the person charged with the commission of a crime cannot be convicted unless *mens rea* on his part is established, although there are many crimes (particularly statutory offences) in which *mens rea* is of no moment.

Messenger-at-arms.—A messenger-at-arms is an officer of both the Court of Session and the sheriff court whose principal functions are connected with the doing of **diligence** (*q.v.*). His functions in Court of Session matters are similar to those of the **Sheriff officer** in the sheriff court. He is appointed by the Lord Lyon King of Arms and with few exceptions messengers-at-arms are also sheriff officers acting in the sheriffdoms for which they are appointed by the sheriff. A list of messengers-at-arms will be found in the *Scottish Law Directory* and the *Parliament House Book*.

Minor.—A minor is a young person who has attained the age of 12 in the case of a girl and 14 in the case of a boy, but who in either case has not attained the age of 18. (Before the Age of Majority (Scotland) Act 1969 came into operation the upper age was 21.) A minor has a legal personality but his or her legal powers and capacities are limited. A minor cannot be a trustee in sequestration or a tutor, curator or judicial factor. (See under each of these headings.) He or she is able to enter into legal transactions including the sale of heritable property with the consent of his or her curator, although a minor (not a **pupil** (*q.v.*)) without a curator or one who has been **forisfamiliated** (*q.v.*) has the same contractual powers as a person of full age. The curator's function is simply to advise on and consent to a contract into which his ward enters but even such a contract is voidable at the minor's instance at any time within the four years immediately following the date when the minor attains majority (see **Quadriennium utile**) if the court is satisfied that what the minor obtained from the transaction was much less than he should reasonably have got. There are exceptions to this rule, however, as for example where a minor represents himself or herself to be a major. A minor has power to raise an action (to which his or her curator, if he has one, must consent) for harm or damage done to him or her. He or she may hold property heritable and moveable and may make a will, disposing of any or all of his or her property.

The minor's parents are his or her natural curators but if either of his or her parents is dead or both are or the survivor is unsuitable to be the curator, some other person may be appointed by the court on the minor's application. If the minor is involved in litigation and has no curator, a **curator ad litem** (*i.e.* for the litigation) must be appointed. It will be plain from the foregoing that there may be hesitation about contracting with a minor who has no curator.

Minute.—The word has several meanings. It refers to one of the documents forming the **process** of an action in court. The minute may set out the position of the party on whose behalf it is put into the process or may deal with some procedural matter with which he is concerned, *e.g.* amending pleadings by requesting that a fact should be sworn to by the other party, or it may simply intimate that the party who puts it into process is abandoning the action. A minute may be lodged by both parties to an action when it is referred to as a joint minute. A recent addition to the meanings of the word is its use in an undefended divorce action to refer to the document put into process by an advocate setting out the evidence given by the pursuer or a witness by way of an **affidavit.**

The plural of the word (minutes) has the less technical meaning of a record kept of the proceedings and the decisions taken at any meeting of an organisation (*e.g.* a company, firm, club or committee).

Missives.—A missive is a writing usually in letter form. Missives of sale are letters which can be proved to have been written by the parties to the transaction (the addition by the signatory above his signature of the words "adopted as holograph" to a typed missive is sufficient proof) or which are in the handwriting of the parties.

The expression is most frequently used in the context of the sale of heritage by private bargain, *i.e.* after advertisement without a public auction where one party offers to purchase from the other (the seller) who accepts the offer. The letters may, instead of being written by the parties themselves, be written on their behalf by their solicitors. Thus completed missives constitute a contract binding on both parties for the sale of land or buildings. Where the land is sold by public auction the procedure is more formal and the conditions of sale of the land or buildings may be found in part in articles of roup and sale (see **Public roup**).

Mortgage.—This is an English term meaning (in English language) a conveyance or other transfer of real or personal estate as security for the repayment of money borrowed. Regrettably it is now commonly used in Scotland as the result mainly of building society, bank and estate agent influence to mean loans made by any of them for the same purpose. The expression chattle mortgage of Canadian origin has happily not yet come into use at all in Scotland.

Mortis causa.—See **Donation mortis causa.**

Motion roll.—The motion roll is one of the rolls for the keeping of which the rules of the Court of Session provide. A motion made by any party in an action before the Court of Session is made by entry in the motion sheet. The entry specifies the terms of the motion and bears the date of enrolment and a certificate that it has been intimated to the other party to the action. All such motions are enrolled for hearing by the court on the second day after the enrolment and if the attendance of counsel is required to move the motion, it is starred in the roll of court in which it appears.

Moveable property (also **Moveables**).—In law, all property that is not heritable is classified as moveable. Where the property can be handled and can move or can be moved it is called "corporeal moveable property". Thus for instance animals, clothing, books, pictures, furniture, machinery, implements, vehicles, aircraft, bank notes and coins are all moveable property. Where the property has an existence recognised by law but no actual physical existence, it is known as "incorporeal moveable property".

Multiplepoinding.—A court action brought actually or nominally by a person who has in his possession moveable property the ownership of which is, as to the whole, a part or parts, in dispute (see **Fund in medio**). Instances are a bank with funds the ownership of which is in doubt, the police who have a stolen car in their possession and the surplus in the hands of a building society after they have sold a house on which a loan they have made has not been repaid. After special procedure, designed to establish who the claimants on the fund, and their respective titles to it, are, the court makes a decree settling the question. The court concerned is that of the area in which the fund *in medio* is lying. This is one of the few cases in which the location of moveables confers jurisdiction on the court of their location. It is not regarded by most other legal systems (none for instance within the EEC) as a ground of jurisdiction.

Multures (pronounced "mooters")—The law of "multures" is (or rather was, for it has ceased to have practical effect) part of the Scots law of thirlage. Thirlage is frequently classified with servitudes but is more accurately an element of feudal tenure. It was the limitation of lands and their inhabitants to particular mills for the grinding of corn with the burden of paying such duties and services as are expressed or implied in the constitution of the right. Multures are the proportion of grain paid to the miller for the grinding of the rest. In earlier times tenants were thirled to the landlord's mill. "Dry" multures was the sum of money paid to the landowner in lieu of a proportion of grain and came into use generally after thirlage ceased to exist in its true form. In so far as payments of multures are now made they are treated and change ownership in much the same way as feuduties — divorced from the land with which they were in past time connected but for the fact that the owner of the land is obliged to make the payment.

Mutatis mutandis.—This means "with the necessary changes". Where, for instance, a document is dealing with the same subject as another and in the same general form, it may be possible to include the wording of the former in the latter, subject only to changes of words or phrases, and thus confer full meaning to the latter.

N

Natural justice.—It is arguable that the one word of this phrase contradicts the other if the two are examined separately. Law being the creation of mankind for the regulation peacefully of his activities in society cannot be natural in the sense of being uncontrived, and justice, if its existence is conceded, is the quality to achieve which the law strives, of being fair, impartial, exact, etc. The phrase has however come in recent times to have another artificial significance connected with hearings of disputes, inquiries and arbitrations. It consists of three main principles; first that a person hearing a case, dispute, arbitration or inquiry must hear both sides or at least give both sides equal opportunity to present their arguments, second that a person should not be or appear to be judge in his own cause, and third that justice must not only be done but also be seen to be done.

Naturalisation.—This has been defined as a right granted to a stranger or **alien** by the authority of Parliament, in virtue of which he acquires the same privileges as if he had been born in the UK. An alien who wishes to become a naturalised British subject must follow the procedure set out in the British Nationality Acts 1948-1965 as amended by the Immigration Act 1971, whereby applications for naturalisation are submitted to the Home Secretary. The Scottish Office has no official function in this sphere.

Negligence.—Broadly, negligence means an act or omission which ignores the care for others required by law. It may be the result of deliberate action or course of action and is not dissimilar therefore from reckless behaviour. It may also be the result of an unintentional breach of duty, as where the conduct was inadequately careful in the circumstances, or, where liability is strict, the conduct may be negligent if it simply fails to prevent injury. Lastly, if the liability is absolute (statute so provides in certain circumstances) the conduct may result in liability simply because the injury required to be prevented has happened at all. Where the conduct which results in injury is either intentional or negligent, the law attaches an element of moral blameworthiness to it which is termed *culpa.*

Negotiable instruments.—Certain kinds of documents evidencing indebtedness or conferring a right to obtain payment of money have, by reason of long-standing commercial usage, the quality of being negotiable. This imports that (a) the document and the incorporeal moveable right which it embodies, are transferable by delivery alone — a deed assigning the right is not required, and (b) it confers a good title (notwithstanding lack of, or defect in, the title of the transferor) on the transferee who takes in good faith, for value, and without notice of any defect in the title. Examples of negotiable instruments are bills of exchange, promissory notes (including banknotes), cheques, treasury bills, share warrants issued "to bearer", bankers' drafts and dividend warrants. Postal orders, share certificates, pension receipts, letters of credit and deposit receipts are not negotiable instruments.

Nemine contradicente.—A phrase reduced in practice to *nem. con.*, used when voting takes place on a formal occasion (a conference, meeting of a governing body, trustees, etc.) and a proposition is before the meeting for decision. If the proposition is accepted unanimously it is said to have been carried *nem. con., i.e.* without a dissenter.

Next-of-kin.—From the legal point of view this phrase means only "the class of relatives entitled at common law to succeed to moveable estate on the death of the owner." The phrase is, however, frequently used in a context in which a particular person is being identified, although in that context it is of little legal force. A form authorising the performance in hospital of a surgical operation for instance, asks for the name of the next-of-kin of the person to be operated on. This is of little legal worth. It is usual for the person named as next-of-kin in such circumstances to be the spouse or, if he or she has no spouse, the person with whom he or she is living or a near relative. If the patient is a minor or a young person living with his parents one of the parents will be named. The person named may be contacted in case of emergency but cannot authorise or homologate any action proposed to be taken or already taken. The relatives as a whole may do so along with the person concerned if he is still alive.

Nobile officium.—The *nobile officium* is the ultimate residual equitable power of the Court of Session (exercised normally by the Inner House of the court) to provide a remedy where the existing law does not provide one or where injustice would result from the strict application of the law. In modern times this power is used in very exceptional circumstances only and is in practice exercised only where there is precedent or close analogy. The main classes of case where the court has exercised its *nobile officium* are those where omissions or defects in statutes or statutory procedure have been found, where there have been omissions in deeds or writings particularly in relation to trusts, where there has been need for the appointment of trustees or for the settlement of schemes in charitable trusts (technically known as *cy-près* schemes), where appointments, of an interim nature, to public offices have had to be made and where authority to do something, particularly with regard to public records, has been required.

Nolle prosequi.—This is an English legal term meaning "unwilling to prosecute". It is a formal averment and refers, but for one special criminal instance, to civil proceedings and effects the withdrawal of the cause of action in respect of which it is made. It has no place in Scots law.

Nonage.—Nonage as a general expression means immaturity, or put negatively, not being of full age. In Scots law therefore, as applied to a person, it means a person who is in pupillarity or minority as opposed to a person who, being 18 years of age or more, has attained **majority.**

Non compos mentis.—Of unsound mind; antithesis of **Compos mentis.**

Notarial execution.—Notarial execution is a method by which a deed may be granted notwithstanding the inability of the granter for whatever reason to sign it. (See ss. 18 and 41 of the Conveyancing (Scotland) Act 1924.) It can be carried out only if there are present not only the granter but a notary public or a solicitor or a justice of the peace or, in the case of a will, a parish minister in his own parish or his colleague and successor. (See s. 13 of the Church of Scotland (Property and Endowment) Amendment (Scotland) Act 1933.) The notary public, solicitor, justice of the peace or minister, whichever of them is performing the function in the particular case, must know that the person for whom he acts is the person designed (see **Designation**) as granting the deed, or have that fact affirmed by others, and there must also be present two other persons to act as witnesses. After procedure of a very formal nature laid down by statute has been gone through (the procedure is not dealt with here) the person acting signs the deed and adds a statutory holograph (see **Holograph**) docquet on the last page after which he signs the deed again. The two witnesses sign opposite his signature at both places.

Notary public.—The office of notary public, to which a solicitor may be appointed by the Court of Session, was at one time of great importance having many functions attached to it mainly connected with land transactions. Nowadays for the most part a notary public's functions are concerned with the completion in Scotland of affidavits and other documents giving information required by the authorities of other countries. The person who is to make the affidavit, or to sign the document, is put on oath by the notary public and swears that the information contained in it is true. He then signs and the notary adds his signature thereafter. The notary also has functions in connection with bills of exchange and the signature of documents (including **wills**) by persons who are illiterate or who are physically incapable of writing. A register of all notaries public is kept by the clerk and the agent whose name can be found in the *Scottish Law Directory* and *Parliament House Book.*

Notour bankrupt.—See **Bankruptcy.**

Nova debita.—Literally translated this phrase means "new debts" and it refers in the field of bankruptcy law to debts incurred by the bankrupt after he has become insolvent. It gives expression to an exception to the rule that all the bankrupt's debts must be met out of the whole estate or, to put it another way, that a pecuniary obligation undertaken by a person after he has become bankrupt is not to be met in full. The obligations to which the exception applies are all transactions in which the conveyance or other deed or act of alienation by the bankrupt is granted or done in pursuance of an obligation undertaken for a fair and present value given. The simplest instances are sales for fair price, or loans upon specific security given by the bankrupt in exchange for the advance.

Novodamus.—Translated literally "we give of new". A charter of novodamus was, and may still be, used to make some alteration to the provisions (burdens or other conditions) in the title to heritable property, to correct a mistake in the title or to provide a new title deed where the original has been lost.

Null.—See **Void; Nullity.**

Nullity.—This word has no specific legal meaning except perhaps in relation to declarator of nullity of marriage which is associated with a marriage being void or voidable. Its general meaning is the state of being null or void, want of existence, force or efficacy and it is used in this sense about legal writs, acts or deeds which are ineffective.

O

Obiter dictum.—Obiter means "by the way" or "casually"; *obiter dictum* describes an opinion expressed by a judge upon a matter or point not essential to the decision of the case of the judgment in which the opinion is part. The opinion may, however, though not authoritative be used to assist in the decision of some other case to which it is relevant. Often used in opposition to ratio decidendi (*q. v.*).

Obligationes literis.—*Obligationes literis* are those categories of obligations of great importance which must be constituted in writing. Each must be executed by the granter in the manner required by statute and can be proved only by the terms of the writing. Such a writing proves itself; writs **holograph** (*q.v.*) of the granter or adopted as holograph by him are the equivalent of a solemnly executed writing. Included amongst such writings are contracts relating to heritable property (including purchase and sale), bonds or obligations for the payment of money (see Subscription of Deeds Act 1540), contracts of service for more than one year, cautionary obligations (see **Caution; Guarantee**), and submissions to arbitration. Non-compliance with any rule for authenticating a writing may be cured by **homologation** or *rei interventus*. Proof that such a rule has been complied with is itself subject to rules.

Offence.—See **Indictable offence.**

Ombudsman.—This word is derived from a Scandinavian word meaning "a grievance man". In Scotland there are three offices of a similar kind. One is the **Parliamentary Commissioner for Administration,** the second is the **Commissioner for Local Administration in Scotland,** and the third is the **Heath Service Commissioner for Scotland.** The first office was created by, and the holder is appointed and carries out his duties under, the Parliamentary Commissioner Act 1967; the second was created by, and the holder is appointed and carries out his duties under, Part II of the Local Government (Scotland) Act 1975, and the third under s. 45 of the National Health Service (Scotland) Act 1972.

Open Record.—See **Record.**

Orders in Council.—Orders in Council are made by the Sovereign when in session with the Privy Council. They are made by virtue of the Royal prerogative but their use is confined almost entirely to actings in wartime and to legislation for what remains of the British Colonies. Legislation also confers powers to make **subordinate legislation** by Order in Council. An Order in Council is authenticated by the prefixing of the sign manual, *i.e.* the Sovereign's name written in the Sovereign's own hand.

Ordinary action.—Any civil action raised in the sheriff court which is not a **summary cause** is referred to as an ordinary action. Ordinary actions are for the most part more complex or raise more difficult questions of fact or law than summary causes. But if the sum sued for does not exceed £500 the summary cause procedure must be used. A definition of summary cause, however, makes the meaning of ordinary action more comprehensible.

Outer House.—See **Court of Session.**

P

Panel.—This word refers to a person charged with a crime or offence who has appeared in court to answer to the charge. (See **Accused.**)

Pari passu.—This phrase is used most frequently in relation to creditors of an insolvent estate. It is also used in documents ranking the priority of secured creditors *inter se*. It means "on an equal footing" or "proportionately", and refers to the sharing of whatever assets are available for division between the creditors.

Parliamentary Commissioner for Administration.—The Parliamentary Commissioner for Administration may investigate any action taken in the exercise of administrative functions by or on behalf of any government department or other authority listed in Schedule 2 (as amended) to the Parliamentary Commissioner Act 1967. Before such an investigation may be undertaken a written complaint must be made to the Commissioner by a Member of Parliament to whom the aggrieved person has first complained. In certain cases such an investigation cannot be made (*e.g.* where the aggrieved person has a remedy by proceedings in court). The complaint may be made by an individual (or, if he dies, by his personal representative or a member of his family) or by a body of persons, but not by a local authority or certain other bodies. It must be made within 12 months from the date on which the complainer first had notice of the matters referred to in the complaint and the complainer must be resident in the UK or have been so resident when the action complained of was taken.

The principal officer of the department concerned must be given an opportunity to comment on the allegations made and the investigation must be made in private. The expenses of the complainer may be paid and obstruction of the Commissioner or of any of his officers may be treated as **contempt of court**. The Commissioner has power to call on the minister concerned to give information or produce documents and Crown privilege does not apply. But the Commissioner and officers are bound by the Official Secrets Act 1911 in relation to any information or documents so obtained.

The Commissioner is required to send a report of his investigations to the Member of Parliament concerned and to the principal officer of the department and if he thinks there has been an injustice which has not been or will not be remedied he may make a special report to each House of Parliament. He has no power himself to remedy any such injustice (see also **Ombudsman**).

Parole.—A person who has been convicted of a crime or offence, in respect of which a penalty of a fixed period of imprisonment is imposed, may be released on licence after serving at least 12 months or one-third of the total sentence whichever is the longer, on the recommendation of the Parole Board if the Secretary of State for Scotland agrees.

Partnership.—Partnership is "the relation which subsists between persons carrying on a business in common with a view to profit" (see Partnership Act 1890) (including every trade, occupation or profession). Shareholders in an incorporated body (*e.g.* a company) are not in partnership. Each person who is a member of a partnership must have the legal capacity to enter into a contract of co-partnership. The objects of the partnership must not be illegal nor contrary to public policy. In certain cases, *e.g.* solicitors and dentists, statute provides that a partnership cannot be created unless all the partners are professionally qualified. By custom advocates cannot carry on business in partnership. An association for purposes other than profit is merely a voluntary association and not a partnership and an association for a particular venture, speculation or voyage, for instance, is a joint adventure and not a partnership. There must be at least two persons in a partnership and, except in certain cases (where consent has been given by the Department of Trade), not more than 20.

There are elaborate rules about the constitution of a partnership, for determining its existence, about its legal status as a quasi-legal personality, about the firm (*i.e.* partnership) name, about the powers of individual partners to bind the firm and their liability for partnership debts and obligations. Much of the law is to be found in the 1890 Act, as regards limited partnerships in the Partnership Act 1907 and as regards numbers in the Companies Acts of 1948 and 1967.

Patent.—A patent (also "letters patent") is a grant of monopoly rights in respect of an invention. It is nominally granted by the Crown, but in practice, it is in a form prescribed by Schedule III to the Patent Rules 1958 which is sealed with the seal of the Patent Office. The Comptroller General of Patents, Designs and Trademarks (who is the head of the Patent Office) keeps a register of all patents in force, of assignations and transmissions and other matters affecting patents. An invention is any new or improved manufacture or method of manufacture or any new method or process of testing. Application for a patent must be made to the Patent Office and there are rules about the information to be provided to the office and about many other related matters. The Patent Act 1949 should be consulted.

Patria potestas.—This Latin phrase expresses a feature of Roman law which had real content; it meant the almost unlimited power of control and direction which a Roman father had over his children. In Scots law it means little more than the powers which either parent has as guardian of their child. Most of these powers are mentioned under the headings of **Guardian, Curator, Tutor, Minor** and **Pupil,** and reference should be made to them. Apart from the elements mentioned under these headings there are some others, *e.g.* the power to decide on religious upbringing, the education and discipline of the child (including punishment of a permissible physical nature), but the limits of the *patria potestas* are doubtful, particularly in the field of discipline, and vary, of course, with the age and status of the child.

Pendente lite.—The translation of this expression is "during the dependence of an action" or "so long as an action is before the court". Its significance is that during the period when the action is undecided nothing which is relevant to it factually should be altered. For instance a defender cannot, after the action has begun, impair the rights of the other party by disposing of the property or assets which form the subject of the litigation. It appears, however, that steps may be taken so long as they do not tend to make the right of the creditor or pursuer worse. For instance, where the action relates to the validity of a will left by a deceased person there would be nothing to prevent the taking of such steps as are possible to proceed with the preliminary procedure for winding up the estate of which the will disposes or purports to dispose.

Per capita.—Used in connection with the distribution of an estate on succession, and means that where the property goes to a number of persons in equal shares, no single share is divided amongst several as representing a predecessor. The antithesis is succession *per stirpes* (*q.v.*).

Per curiam.—This Latin tag is used commonly in England but seldom in Scotland. In England it signifies that a decision has been arrived at by the court consisting of one or more judges in a case which has come before it. The negative form *per incuriam* ("in error" or "inadvertently") is more used in Scotland for the most part by lawyers who find it helpful to rely on language difficult for their clients to understand or to avoid admitting openly that something said or advice given by them was unsound.

Periculo petentis.—Literally, at the risk of the party who, in a transaction, is seeking to obtain goods from, or to have work done by, another.

Per se.—Of itself or taken alone.

Per stirpes.—A distribution, *e.g.* of property, *per stirpes* is a division among families according to stocks, that is taking into consideration the representatives of deceased persons who, if they had survived, would themselves have been entitled to a share of the property. The share which the predeceasor would have taken is divided equally between his representatives, *e.g.* the children of a predeceasing son or grandson would take equally between them the share to which their father would have succeeded out of his father's or grandfather's estate.

Periodical allowance.—While this phrase can be used in law to describe any payment which is made at regular intervals by one person to another, the former being under a legal obligation to make the payment, it is specifically used in statute law relating to divorce (see the Divorce (Scotland) Act 1976). Either party to a marriage may, at any time prior to the court granting decree of divorce, no matter which party raises the action, apply to the court for an order for the payment to him or her or for his or her benefit by the other party to the marriage of a periodical payment. Before any such order is made the court will give consideration to the respective means of both parties and to all the circumstances of the case.

A particular periodical payment will cease when the court varies it or upon the re-marriage or death of the person for whose benefit it is paid. The liability will not cease on the death of the person against whom the order was made; it will continue to be payable out of such estate as he or she leaves. Again the re-marriage of the person against whom the order is made does not bring his or her duty to pay the allowance to an end, just as the re-marriage does not bring the duty to pay aliment to the children of the earlier marriage to an end.

Perjury.—Perjury is the crime committed by a person who, when giving evidence on oath or affirmation as a witness in a court, gives evidence which he knows to be false.

Personal bar.—In many circumstances in civil disputes a person may be prevented from establishing what is, on the face of it, his legal right because he is personally barred from doing so. In general the doctrine of personal bar (which, in England is termed **estoppel**) is designed to ensure that a person should not be able to enforce claims which he has already, expressly or by implication, abandoned. "Where A has by his words or conduct justified B in believing that a certain state of facts exists and B has acted on such belief to his prejudice A is not permitted to affirm against B that a different state of facts existed at the same time" (from a judgment by Lord Birkenhead). Words so used are presumed to have their ordinary meaning.

Pertinents.—Pertinents, or more commonly, parts and pertinents, is an expression used in conveyances of land and buildings. It may be said to comprise everything which, from its close connection with the land or buildings being conveyed, passes to the purchaser as an accessory of the land or buildings. It would be no matter if the word or words were omitted since a conveyance of the land or buildings includes the parts and pertinents. But the words nonetheless usually appear in conveyances and are convenient for expressing rights accessory to the land.

Plea.—The final section of a summons by which a civil action is raised in the Court of Session or of an initial writ in the sheriff court contains a brief statement of the legal grounds, which, if the facts are proved, would entitle the pursuer to the remedy he seeks or, in other words, to decree in his favour. The word is used more generally and loosely to mean a lawsuit or the answer which an accused makes to a charge in a criminal case or a defender in a civil case.

Plea in mitigation.—This is not strictly a legal expression. It is used to describe what a person who pleads guilty to, or is found guilty of, the commission of a crime or offence may say before sentence is passed by the judge. He or the lawyer acting for him may plead that there are good reasons why something less than the maximum penalty should be imposed or that a monetary penalty (and no period of imprisonment) should be imposed or even that the sentence should be an admonition, because, for example, the accused is of good character or the offence was trifling.

Pleadings.—The pleadings in civil actions either in the Court of Session or the sheriff court are the written allegations, admissions and denials of each party. In the case of an action in the Court of Session the pleadings appear in the condescendence which forms part of the summons by which the action was initiated, in a sheriff court action they are part of the initial writ which began the action. After the record has been closed the pleadings are complete. The singular form of the word is used as a verb to signify what the lawyer does when he appears in court to present and argue the case (see **Open record**).

Poinding (pronounced "pinding").—Poinding is part of the process of enforcing a decree of court, that is of doing **diligence.** After a **charge** (*q.v.*) has been served on a debtor and the debtor has not paid the sum due before the expiry of the days of charge the creditor on whose behalf the charge has been served may request a **sheriff officer** or a **messenger-at-**

74

arms to poind (impound) moveable goods (furniture, equipment, vehicles, etc.) belonging to the debtor and in his possession of such value as, if sold by auction, would produce sufficient funds to meet the sum, or some part of the sum, due. Goods in the premises occupied by the debtor but which do not belong to him cannot be poinded to meet his debts. Such goods are those belonging to other members of the family, to lodgers or visitors, or goods which are the subject of a hire purchase agreement entered into by the debtor. Moreover, certain goods belonging to the debtor cannot be poinded. Included in that category are tools of the debtor's trade and personal belongings and household goods necessary for the purpose of ordinary living. Caravans which are moveable are poindable but those fixed to the ground are heritable and thus not poindable.

Poinding is carried out by the sheriff officer or messenger-at-arms in the presence of a witness and a valuator (two if the cause is not a summary cause) and the officer or messenger makes an inventory of the goods poinded. The valuator appraises the value of the goods and enters the appraised value in the inventory, a copy of which he hands to the debtor. The officer or messenger returns his execution of poinding signed by himself and the witnesses to the clerk of court. The execution of poinding is a **probative document.** At or after the poinding the debtor may still pay the sum due. The goods remain in his possession but he must not dispose of them or remove them from the premises where they were poinded. The next step after poinding, if the debt is not settled, is for the creditor to obtain authority from the court to sell the poinded goods.

Poinding of the ground.—This is an action which can be raised only by the creditor to whom a debt secured over land (*e.g.* a **feu duty** or a **standard security**) is due. The effect of the granting of a decree, if obtained, in such circumstances is to attach all the moveables on the ground belonging to the debtor but only for payment of arrears of rent and of rent for the period during which the action is raised.

Police powers.—(to require certain persons to identify themselves, etc). A constable may require a person, whom he has reasonable grounds for suspecting to have committed, or to be committing, an offence, to give information identifying himself (see s. 1 of the Criminal Justice (Scotland) Act 1980). Supplementary powers about questioning, detaining and arresting a person, searching a person for weapons and ascertaining whether a person is under the influence of alcohol are conferred by ss. 2-5 of the same Act.

Post hoc ergo propter hoc.—Literally "after this therefore because of this". An instance of false reasoning which proceeds by saying that because a result has post-dated an event, the occurrence of the event was responsible for the result.

Power of attorney.—A power of attorney granted by one person to another enables the other to conduct the whole of the granter's affairs or such of them as are specified in the deed granting the power. It may be cancelled at any time by either party giving notice in writing to the other. In certain circumstances (*e.g.* if a power is granted after one has already

75

been given in the same terms) cancellation is implied. The word "attorney" used here is derived from its use for identification of a person legally qualified to act for another. (See **Mandate**). An instrument may be proved to have created a power of attorney by any of the means set out in s. 3 of the Powers of Attorney Act 1971. One is by means of a photocopy in facsimile and another by a copy signed by the donor and certified by a solicitor or stockbroker.

Praepositura.—This is a form of agency. It is used now almost exclusively in relation to husband and wife. It is presumed from cohabitation that the wife, who is *praeposita rebus domesticis* (responsible for administration of domestic matters) has her husband's authority in all such matters. The authority extends only to contracts for necessaries — such as goods and services necessary to maintain the home — but does not extend to transactions unconnected with the management of the household. The husband may terminate his wife's authority by express intimation to suppliers but not by general advertisement. He may also terminate it by execution of letters of inhibition against his wife which, when recorded in the Register of Inhibitions and Adjudications, is effective even if not known to the supplier.

Precedent.—A precedent is an example — the judgment of a court or a proposition of law — which may, and in some instances must, be followed. The word is used principally, but by no means exclusively, to indicate one of the two following things:

(1) a decision by a court of law cited in support of any legal proposition which is being contended for. A prior decision of the House of Lords is binding on all inferior courts. In Scotland a decision of the High Court of Justiciary in a criminal matter or by the Court of Session in a civil matter is binding on the sheriff in a case in which a similar criminal or, as the case may be, civil issue arises — only an Act of Parliament can alter such a binding decision; or

(2) Acts of Parliament, completed deeds, wills, security documents and written pleadings (or drafts of them) which may serve as patterns (*i.e.* precedents) for future draftsmen and conveyancers. Other documents also fall into this class.

Precognition.—A precognition is a preliminary examination of a person who may be required to give evidence in a criminal trial or civil proof. The purpose of obtaining a precognition is to have knowledge in advance of the trial or proof of the evidence the witness will be able to give about facts which are likely to emerge as relevant and which will require to be proved. The likely evidence is set out in a document, also called a "precognition", but, unlike the position in England, the witness does not have to sign the precognition and is not bound to give his evidence exactly as recorded in it.

Precognosce.—See **Precognition.**

Prescription.—Prescription is a term used to describe the effect of the passing of time on rights to which a person is entitled or on obligations which he owes to others. The legal effect of prescription may be either to establish rights (principally servitudes and public rights of way) or fortify existing rights (the positive prescription) or to extinguish rights or obligations (the negative prescription). Until Part I of the Prescription and Limitation (Scotland) Act 1973 came into operation on 25 July 1976 there was a variety of periods laid down by statutes passed over the centuries from 1469 onwards dealing with both the positive and negative prescriptions. One effect of the 1973 Act was to reduce to a small number the wide variety of negative prescriptive periods.

The prescriptive periods now in existence are briefly:

(1) The "positive" prescription of ten years. The prescriptive period fortifies a bad or defective title to land if the land has been possessed and possession has been founded on a recorded deed sufficient to constitute in favour of a person a title in the particular land, and if during the ten years the land has been possessed by that person or by him and his successors continuously, openly, peaceably and without judicial interference. While the ten-year period demands possession founded on a recorded title, recording is unnecessary in the case of a title to (a) an interest under a lease, (b) any interest in **allodial** land, and (c) any other interest where the title to that interest would have been a good foundation for prescription under the law in force before the 1973 Act came into operation. In any such case (where the title is in fact unrecorded) the prescriptive period is 20 years.

There are also certain other cases where the question at issue is more often whether a right has been created rather than whether a bad or defective title has been fortified. In such cases the period of positive prescription is 20 years. They are: (a) where a right to foreshore or salmon fishing is pleaded against the Crown; (b) where the constitution by use alone of a positive servitude over land is being contended for or the fortification of a written title to a servitude (whether recorded or not) is being sought; and (c) the constitution by public use of a right-of-way is being contended for.

(2) The "long negative" prescription extinguishes obligations of any kind and any right relating to property (except where the obligation or right is imprescriptible) unless a claim to the obligation or right has been relevantly made or the subsistence of the obligation has been acknowledged or the right has been exercised within a period of 20 years (see ss. 6 to 8 of and Schedules 1, 2 and 3 to the 1973 Act). It remains competent, however, after the 20-year period has expired to challenge a deed on the ground that it is a forgery or is intrinsically null (e.g. because there was no power to grant it) and to establish a right to stolen property or property which cannot be sold but which was wrongly disposed of.

(3) The "five years prescription period" extinguishes obligations to pay money (including instalments of interest, feuduty, ground annual and rent), obligations arising from or by reason of breach of contract or promise (unless constituted or evidenced by a deed which is proof itself of the formation of the contract or the giving of the promise), obligations to make **reparation** (other than for personal injury or death), obligations of **restitution** and obligations of accounting (see **Count reckoning and payment**). These are among the more important categories of obligations

extinguished after five years.

In certain cases a statute dealing with specific subject-matter (*e.g.* income tax) may create its own "domestic" period during which a right or claim is to be enforceable, and s. 12 of the 1973 Act provides that its provisions are not to affect (that is, reduce) any such "domestic" period where it is created in a statute passed before the passing of the 1973 Act. The 1973 Act was amended in certain respects by s. 23 of the Law Reform (Miscellaneous Provisions) (Scotland) Act 1980.

Prior rights.—From 1911 (when the conception of prior rights was first introduced by statute into Scots law) until 10 September 1964 (when the Succession (Scotland) Act 1964 came into operation), the only prior right in the law of succession was the right of a widow (whose husband died intestate without leaving **legitimate issue**) to the whole of his estate heritable and moveable if not exceeding £500. The right was in addition and in priority to **legal rights** (*q.v.*) and was extended to widowers, to cases of partial intestacy and raised to £5,000 in 1959. The effect of the introduction of the 1911 provisions and the extension were in many cases to exclude the rules of intestate succession because the amount of the estate was less than £500. The right was postponed to the rights of creditors and did not apply where a will disposed of the whole estate.

The 1964 Act replaced these provisions with another scheme of prior rights where the deceased died wholly or partially intestate. These rights have priority over all legal rights but do not affect succession to any title, coat-of-arms, honour or dignity transmissible on the death of the holder (see **Legal rights**). The prior rights are:

(1) If the intestate estate includes an interest as owner or tenant (not being a tenancy to which the Rent Act 1971 applies) in any dwellinghouse including part of a building occupied (at the date of the deceased's death) as a separate dwelling (and any garden or ground attached) in which the surviving spouse was resident at the date of the death, that spouse is entitled (a) to the dwelling and garden or ground where its value does not exceed £30,000 or (b) to the value (where it does not exceed £30,000) of both if the dwellinghouse forms part of the subjects included in a lease under which the deceased was the tenant or formed the whole or part of the subjects used by the deceased for carrying on a trade, profession or occupation (*e.g.* farming) and the value of the whole would be likely to be substantially diminished if the dwellinghouse were disposed of otherwise than with the assets of the trade, profession or occupation; or (c) in any other case to a sum of £30,000. Where the deceased had two or more dwellinghouses, the right applies only to the one which the surviving spouse elects to take. The surviving spouse in all three instances, takes the interest subject to any heritable debt secured over it (see s. 8 of the Succession (Scotland) Act 1964 as amended by s. 1 (1) (a) of the Succession (Scotland) Act 1973).

(2) The surviving spouse is also entitled, where the intestate estate includes the furniture and plenishings of a dwellinghouse in which the surviving spouse was ordinarily resident at the date

of death of the deceased (whether or not the dwellinghouse is comprised in the intestate estate) to the whole of the furniture and the plenishings but not heirlooms (all these words are defined in the Act) if their value does not exceed £8,000 or, in any other case, such part of them as does not exceed £8,000 in value. If there are two or more dwellinghouses involved, the surviving spouse can elect to which one of them this provision will apply. Any dispute about the value of the property to which (1) or (2) apply is to be settled by arbitration.

(3) The surviving spouse is entitled, if the deceased is survived by **issue** (*q.v.*) to £8,000 or, if not survived by issue to £16,000 (see Prior Rights of Surviving Spouse (Scotland) Order 1977.) The value of any legacy left to the surviving spouse is taken into account in arriving at the sum of £8,000 or, as the case may be, £16,000.

If the whole of the intestate estate is less than the sum to which the surviving spouse is entitled, she takes the whole. If the deceased left a will disposing of the whole or part of his estate, the surviving spouse has no title to receive any part of the £8,000 or the £16,000 out of the estate so disposed of even if the balance left over is less than the one or the other. (See **Legal Rights; Spouse; Succession.**)

Private Act.—A Private Act of Parliament is a statute which enables a person or persons, a public company or corporation, a local authority or other similar body to do something or carry on some activity which is for his, her or their constituents' particular interest or benefit. The name is given to such an Act to distinguish it from a measure enacted by Parliament as a matter of public policy in which the whole community is interested. The Interpretation Act 1889 provides that every Act of Parliament is to be treated as a Public Act unless there is an express declaration to the contrary in the Act. The most common method of securing private legislation in Scotland is by means of an order made under the Private Legislation Procedure (Scotland) Act 1936 which is given statutory effect by a short formal Act of Parliament to which the order is an appendix. This is a device to enable statutory powers to be conferred by procedure carried out in Scotland. In theory Acts of Parliament can be passed only in Parliament at Westminster.

Privilege.—This word is used in a number of legal contexts. In its widest sense it means that which is granted or allowed to any person or class of persons either against or beyond the course of ordinary law. There are two broad divisions or categories of privilege — absolute privilege and qualified privilege.

In the case of absolute privilege for reasons of public policy communications whether oral or written made in certain circumstances cannot provide the foundation for an action in court even if defamatory. It is a question of law whether the circumstances confer absolute privilege; these circumstances are not settled but the courts are not willing to go beyond existing precedent. They include statements made in Parliament, reports thereof in *Hansard* and fair and accurate official communications between officers of state and notifications in the *Gazette* of acts of state. All statements made in the course of judicial

79

proceedings (including special jurisdiction, quasi-judicial functions but not administrative functions such as, it is thought, inquiries under the Planning Acts) with limited exceptions, are absolutely privileged, as are statements made by the Lord Advocate or procurators fiscal in the course of their official duties and probably all documents (including decrees) issued by the courts.

Qualified privilege is a different matter. A person may in certain circumstances without enjoying absolute privilege, communicate what is or may be defamatory but will not incur liability in damages unless it can be shown that he did so because of express or actual malice in making the communication. Whether qualified privilege applies in any particular circumstances is a question of law. The circumstances in which it does apply are not settled and, if there is no precedent available, the court may have regard to changes in circumstances which, they may think, render it applicable. Qualified privilege applies also where a person makes a statement honestly believing it to be made in discharge of a public or private duty or for the protection of some other person's interests or, if the communication is made in good faith, between persons having a common interest. for instance, a master speaking to his servant about the latter's colleagues or a banker expressing a view about a client's financial position. Certain published reports are also privileged (fair and accurate press reports of Parliamentary proceedings have already been mentioned and broadcast reports are in the same position). Moreover a statement is not defamatory if it is **fair comment.**

Apart from these meanings of the word privilege there are many others. The difference between rights of way or passage and privilege of *e.g.* skating, curling, or walking, is mentioned under the headings **Right of way** and **Servitude** (*q.v.*). There are privileged debts and privileged writings, *e.g.* a writing (or deed) which requires one witness only, deeds which require no witnesses (*e.g.* those executed on behalf of a company) and deeds authenticated by mark and not by signature.

Probate.—This term has no place in Scots law. In English law it means the exhibiting and proving of a will in the High Court. The nearest Scottish equivalent is "confirmation".

Probation.—In certain circumstances where a person appears before a court charged with an offence (usually of a minor character) of which he is found guilty, the court, instead of sentencing him (*e.g.* imposing a penalty of imprisonment) may make a probation order which requires him to be under the supervision of a social worker for a period of one to three years.

Probative.—This word means, simply, "affording proof". Thus a probative document is one which, because of certain features — proper preparation and production, formal signature and witnessing — affords proof at least on the face of it, of its contents.

Pro bono publico.—For the good, advantage or benefit of the public, people at large or citizens. Used in a general sense and without precision.

Proceedings.—When used in relation to a court action, this word means all that happens from the time the action is begun until it is decided by the court.

Process.—The whole papers relating to a civil action lodged in court (see also **Adjustments; Open record**).

Procurator.—A rather out-of-date name for a solicitor. Still used, however, to refer to a lawyer who specialises in conducting cases in the sheriff court.

Procurator fiscal.—The procurators fiscal are the public prosecutors in the sheriff court and in the district court and are full-time civil servants. They must be either solicitors or advocates. The police report the details of any crime or offence to the procurator fiscal of the area where it was committed. The fiscal has discretion whether or not to prosecute subject to the direction and control of the **Crown Office.** While the procurator fiscal carries out the day-to-day work of prosecution in the sheriff court in which he is the prosecutor, the Lord Advocate, as principal law officer of the Crown in Scotland, carries the ultimate responsibility for all prosecutions. The procurator fiscal is also responsible for instituting fatal accident inquiries before the sheriff (*i.e.* inquiries into sudden or suspicious deaths normally where no prosecution takes place) and may be concerned in similar inquiries concerning fires. There are no coroners in Scotland.

Production.—A document or article of any sort lodged in or made available to the court by one or other of the parties to an action in the court is termed a production. Its use is as part, or as an adminicle of the evidence by which the party seeks to prove or defend the case. It may be anything from a thimble to a traction engine or a scrap of paper to a probative document.

Pro forma.—Literally for form's sake or "as a matter of form". As a noun, used to describe a document for use in particular circumstances (*e.g.* when making a claim of some sort), frequently printed with blanks for completion.

Prohibition notice.—This is a notice served (given) under s. 22 of the Health and Safety at Work etc. Act 1974 by an inspector appointed under s. 19 of the Act by the Health and Safety Executive or by any other authority responsible for the enforcement of the provisions of Part I of the Act or of any of the regulations mentioned under the note on **Improvement notice** (*q.v.*). The notice is served on any person in whose case the inspector is of opinion that property (land, buildings, machinery, etc.) for the maintenance of which that person is responsible involves, or potentially involves a risk of serious personal injury to any person rightfully on or using or carrying on activities on property. The notice must contain a statement of the inspector's opinion, and specify certain other matters mentioned in the Act which include remedial action to be taken. Directions given by the notice will take effect immediately if the inspector states that in his opinion there is or will be imminent risk of serious personal injury; otherwise they take effect at the end of the period specified in the notice.

Pro indiviso.—This Latin phrase means little more than "in an undivided state" and is most frequently applied to land owned by several persons in common though not necessarily in equal shares. The land is possessed undivided but each owner has his own separate title to a fraction of the undivided whole. On the death of any one owner his share does not pass to the others but to the person or persons beneficially entitled to it as his successor or successors. He can sell his share and bequeath it by will but actions relating to the land (or any part of it) must be raised or defended by all the owners in common.

Promissory note.—"A promissory note is an unconditional promise in writing made by one person to another, signed by the maker engaging to pay on demand or at a fixed or determinable future time a sum certain in money, to or to the order of a specified person or to bearer." (This definition is to be found in s. 88 of the Bills of Exchange Act 1882).

Proof.—In general this word means simply that which proves or establishes the truth of anything, the first act or process of proving or showing something to be true evidence which convinces the mind and goes towards determining a problem. Scots law also uses it as being the hearing of a civil cause by a judge without a jury. To "lead proof" means to provide evidence for the judge.

Pro rata.—Where two or more persons are bound on the one part in a contract, each is, *prima facie,* bound for his share only, that is, *pro rata.* Similarly, joint creditors are entitled only to a *pro rata* share of the debt due to all of them. Also proportionally.

Prout de jure.—All matters of fact which require to be proved in civil proceedings (apart from those which can be proved only by written evidence) may in general be proved by oral or by written evidence or by a combination of either or both of these with **real evidence** or may be referred to the oath of the opponent. Proof of such a nature is described by the Latin tag *prout de jure* which can be translated roughly as "any means permitted by law".

Public roup or **Roup and Sale.**—"Roup" is a Scottish word meaning a sale by auction or to sell by auction. Public roup thus means a sale by auction which any member of the public may attend and has a right to bid for whatever is put up for sale, each bid exceeding the last. The expression is commonly used in connection with the sale of heritage. In such a case Articles of **Roup and Sale** are prepared by the seller's solicitor. The Articles contain the conditions subject to which the sale is made, a description of the subjects sold and they may be accompanied by a sealed letter which contains a statement of the reserve price, *i.e.* the price below which the subjects will not be sold.

Pupil.—A pupil is a young person who has not attained the age of 12 years if a girl, or 14 if a boy. Her or his legal personality is strictly limited. It has indeed been said that a pupil has no legal personality, but this, if correct, applies in the case of civil law only. Certain elements of criminal law apply to a pupil whose age is under eight years (*e.g.* see the Children and Young Persons (Scotland) Act 1973 as amended by the Social Work (Scotland) Act 1968). She or he has no contractual capacity, any contract must be entered into by her or his tutor on her or his behalf. But any such contract is open to challenge by the child until four years after he or she has attained 18 years of age. (See **Quadriennium utile.**) Money lent to a pupil may be recovered so far as used for his or her benefit and if necessaries are sold and delivered to the pupil she or he must pay a reasonable price for them. She or he has no power to sue for wrong done to her or him nor any liability to be sued. Property may be held by the pupil but will be administered by the tutor. An action in court by the pupil without his tutor is incompetent and a decree given against one without his tutor can be rendered ineffective.

Pursuer.—The pursuer is the person who takes steps to raise, begin or bring a civil action in court or who has already done so. The first step taken by the pursuer is the lodging in court of a document usually termed a summons or initial writ. If the action is one which requires the presentation of a petition to the court the "pursuer" is called the "petitioner". The English term for "pursuer" is "plaintiff".

Putative father.—This expression means the man who is reputed or commonly supposed to be the father of an illegitimate child. It is used as a term of law in England but in Scotland has little more than a colloquial significance.

Q

Quadriennium utile.—This Latin phrase gives expression to the rule of Scots law that contracts entered into by a minor are **voidable** at his or her instance until four years after he or she has attained majority, on proof of his minority at the time the contract was entered into and of the contract having been considerably to his detriment, loss or injury (enorm lesion). (See **Lesion enorm.**) This is derived from Roman law and the minor's heirs, creditors or assignees also may apply to the court to have the contract declared **void** (q.v.). (See also **Pupil; Minor; Guardian; Tutor; Declarator.**)

Quantum lucratus.—Literally "as much as has been gained". Unlike *quantum meruit,* this phrase means that a person has been enriched (*e.g.* by inheritance) without having done anything to earn what he has gained.

Quantum meruit.—Literally, (*"tantum"* being understood), as much as he has earned; a *quantum meruit* may be sued for where work has been done, obviously not for nothing, but where the amount has not been fixed by contract.

Quantum valeat.—Whatever value it may have; for as much as it is worth. A payment will be made to a person in respect of work done for what the work is worth even where the contract has not specified the price or rate for the job.

Quasi.—This word is seldom used by itself. Quasi-contract, for instance, means that the arrangement entered into between two people, while in appearance a contract, is no more than a settlement from the circumstances of which the existence of a legal obligation can be inferred. Quasi-delict is another example.

Queen's and Lord Treasurer's Remembrancer.—The person appointed to this official post was formerly the general administrator of the Crown's revenues in Scotland. It is an ancient office, the functions of which have been transferred in very recent times to other departments, many relating to salaries and expenses of the Lord Advocate's functions and those of his Departments and the collection of certain fines to the Crown Office.

Quid pro quo.—A compensation or the giving of a thing for another thing of like value.

Quoad ultra.—This phrase is much used in the written pleadings in civil actions. The paragraph of a condescendence may read for instance that one averment (made by the opposer) is admitted as being correct but **quoad ultra,** *i.e.* as for the rest, none is admitted or all are denied.

Quorum.—The word is used in the rules etc., of an organisation to establish the minimum number of persons that must be present at any meeting of the organisation for the disposal of business (*e.g.* in Parliament) to give the business disposed of legal effect.

R

Ratio decidendi.—This Latin phrase is often used in opposition to **obiter dictum** and literally translated means the reason of the decision. The more sophisticated meaning of *ratio* is the principle of law underlying and justifying the decision in any case, the proposition of law which can be deduced from it or for which it is an authority. Where the *ratio* provides authority it can be used to decide a later case to the circumstances of which it is in point.

Re mercatoria.—Documents *in re mercatoria* include all variety of engagements, **mandates** or other writs creating an agency agreement. It further includes the generality of acknowledgements which the carrying on of trade requires, including bills of exchange, promissory notes, cheques, orders for goods, guarantees, offers and acceptances to sell or buy merchandise or transport it from place to place. Common law has settled that, for the convenience of business, contracts *in re mercatoria* are binding though not solemnly authenticated. They may be signed, initialled, signed by an agent or by facsimile signature or even by mark if this is the usual mode of authentication used by the particular person. They thus do not need to be holograph or bear the signature of witnesses and may be proved by any legal means. They also prove their own date.

Real evidence.—A definition of this term which is logical could not be adhered to. If the definition "evidence derived from things" were used, the things themselves would inevitably be treated as evidence. If the definition were "anything . . . which is examined by the tribunal" things on which witnesses form opinions but which the tribunal have not inspected because they cannot be moved or have perished would be excluded. The term must therefore be used broadly to include both a thing, which may be a human being, any features of a thing which may be significant and the inferences which may be drawn from the existence of the thing. Broken glass and dried mud left on a road after a road traffic accident and their exact position on the road are real evidence. So is an exclamation which forms part of the circumstances (*res gestae*) and if the accused ran away from the scene of the accident that also is real evidence.

Receiver.—The holder of a **floating charge** on the property of a company or the court on the application of the holder may, on the occurrence of certain events, appoint a receiver of the company's property subject to the charge. It must be made known that he has been appointed and he must make an annual report of his actings to the Registrar of Companies, to the company itself and to certain other persons. His powers are set out in the instrument of appointment and in the Companies (Floating Charges and Receivers) (Scotland) Act 1972. He is the agent of the company and, unless a contract into which he enters otherwise provides, he becomes personally liable under it. Preferential claims are settled by him before he makes any payment to the holder of the floating charge and he thereafter distributes the balance amongst any other claimants and may apply to the court for directions in the performance of any of his functions.

Record.—A civil action in the Court of Session is begun when one litigant serves on the other litigant a summons and lodges a copy in the offices of court. The summons contains amongst a number of other provisions, a detailed statement of the facts upon which the pursuer relies, called the **''condescendence''**, and lastly the **pleas-in-law** which the pursuer says entitle him to the remedy he seeks. The defender thereafter has a chance to put forward his statement of the facts and the pleas-in-law supporting his argument. Thereafter both parties are given a chance of adjusting their statements of fact and their pleas. The record then consists of the summons and adjustments and the parties' pleadings and the whole are described as the "open record" so long as the court permits continuation of this stage of the action to enable further adjustments to be made. When adjustment is complete, the court closes the record — hence "closed record". In an ordinary action in the sheriff court "open record" has the same meaning.

"Record" has a number of other meanings, one of which is the list and report of the stock, crop, equipment, buildings, fencing and condition of the soil on a farm, the working of which is changing hands. The record is made up by an expert agreed upon by the outgoing and incoming farmer.

Recorded.—Technically used to indicate that a deed has been entered in one of the official registers (*e.g.* the Register of Sasines). The person to whom heritage is transferred whether on sale or otherwise does not have full ownership of (*i.e.* is not **vested** in) the property until the deed effecting the transfer has been recorded in the Register of Sasines. Similarly, a **standard security** does not become effective until recorded nor does a decree of **inhibition** or **adjudication.**

Recourse.—As a legal term this word has a number of meanings. For instance, it describes the right which every person has to apply to the court to have his legal position decided in any matter. It also means the right which a person who is the assignee of, say, a right under a contract may have, should he gain nothing by the assignation, to look to the assignor to make good the unimplemented portion of the right.

Reddendo.—This word means the duty or service to be paid or rendered by the vassal to his superior under a feudal writ. The term is of no great significance in modern times. (See **Feu.**)

Reduction, action of.—The object of an action of reduction is to have a deed, decree or other writing of a civil nature which is to the prejudice of the person (pursuer) who initiates the action "declared null". The action can be raised strictly only in the Court of Session, who have power to annul the decree of any inferior court and even its own decrees. If a deed is produced and relied on in a process in the sheriff court, the sheriff has jurisdiction to decide, for that process only, whether the deed is valid or not. The decision of an arbiter (*i.e.* a decree arbitral) may also be reduced by the Court of Session.

It should be noted however that no act of the Crown (which includes all government departments) can be annulled — this is part of the rule that the King can do no wrong. If it is sought to question whether something a government department has done is *ultra vires* (*e.g.* a provision in subordinate legislation) the only remedy is by action of declarator. The Crown Proceedings Act 1947 should be examined.

Redundancy.—Redundancy is, in general terms, the state or quality of being redundant, that is superfluous, or no longer needed. It is most frequently used in modern times in relation to employment where there is a decrease in the work required to be done. Statutory redundancy payments were introduced by the Redundancy Payments Act 1965 and the provisions about them are now to be found in Part VI of the Employment Protection (Consolidation) Act 1978, which is devoted exclusively to the matter. Section 81 (2) of the Act should be looked at.

In construing s. 81, the business of the employer together with the business or businesses of his associated employers are to be treated as "the business", "cease" means cease permanently or temporarily and from whatsoever cause and "diminish" has a corresponding meaning.

A person who has been employed for two years ending with the relevant date (defined in s. 90 of the 1978 Act) and is dismissed by reason of redundancy or is laid off or kept on short-time to the extent specified in s. 88 (1) is entitled to receive from the employer a redundancy payment calculated in accordance with the provisions of the Act (see ss. 103 and 109). The provisions about redundancy as a whole are complex. Advice may be obtained from the Advisory Conciliation and Arbitration Service about them.

Re-engagement.—Where an industrial tribunal finds that an employee has been unfairly dismissed, the tribunal may make an order under s. 69 of the Employment Protection (Consolidation) Act 1978 requiring the employer either to reinstate (see **Reinstatement**) or to re-engage the employee. An order for re-engagement requires that the employee be engaged by the employer (or his successor, or associated employer) in employment comparable to that from which he was dismissed or in other suitable employment. The order must specify the terms on which re-engagement is to take place (see s. 69 (4) of the

1978 Act).

In exercising its discretion the tribunal first consider whether to make an order for reinstatement and in so doing take account of matters set out in the Act (see s. 69 (5)). These matters include whether the employee wishes to be reinstated, whether it is practicable for the employer to reinstate him and, where the employee caused, or contributed to some extent to the dismissal, whether it would be just to order his reinstatement.

If the tribunal decides not to make an order for reinstatement it shall then consider (see s. 69 (6)) whether to make an order for re-engagement and, if so, on what terms, and any wish expressed by the employee as to the nature of the order to be made is to be taken into account. The same considerations are to be taken into account with appropriate substitutions of words as are taken into account where reinstatement is being considered. Unless there was a contributory fault by the employee the tribunal will, if it orders re-engagement, do so on terms as favourable, so far as reasonably practicable, as would result from an order for reinstatement.

Regalia majora.—The *regalia* are rights in land and other subjects which belong to the Crown. The *regalia majora* are such of those rights as are held for the benefit of the people at large and cannot be conveyed or otherwise disposed of by the Crown unless, in some special instances, with the consent of Parliament. The former include the sea within territorial limits (three miles roughly from the land) which is held in trust for the purposes of national defence and the carrying on of trade. The right includes free navigation, fishing, jurisdiction and search. Navigable rivers are in the same position for public use and passage. The bed of the sea below low-water mark is also inalienable except, probably, insofar as its use is required to make piers, ports, or harbours. The Royal prerogative and the paramount superiority over all feudal lands are inseparable from the Royal dignity. A right to moorings on the sea bed cannot be acquired by the public except by a grant from the Crown. Wrecks belong to the Crown and so do large whales in territorial waters and, possibly, swans.

Regalia minora.—The *regalia minora* are rights which belong to the Crown but which can be made over to members of the public. They include the seashore (between high and low water marks of ordinary spring tides) but the Crown cannot diminish the right of the public to use the shore for beaching boats, and recreation such as bathing and shooting wildfowl (except within a nature reserve). Sea salmon fishings are, as also, it is thought, are lobster fishings, taking oysters, mussels and clams (scallops) from sea beds. Trout or other fresh water fishing (except salmon and sea trout) and fresh water shell-fish are not part of the regalia; they go with the owner of the solum of the loch or river in which they are found.

Register of Sasines.—The word sasine in earlier times meant the seizing or placing of a person in possession of land. The register was of such land. In 1617 the Registration Act, replacing earlier legislation, provided that every instrument of sasine (the document which recorded the transfer of the land) and writs relating to redeemable rights in land were to be recorded in a public general register in Edinburgh within 60 days of sasine. There were originally two registers, the General Register in which deeds relating to land anywhere in Scotland could be recorded and the Particular Register for deeds which dealt with land lying in particular sheriffdoms and districts within them. Over the years there were many changes made in the methods to be used in registration and the deeds to be used for transferring land. Instruments of sasine were abolished and the granting of dispositions and feu charters for instance were relied on without further procedure. The Land Registers (Scotland) Act 1869 discontinued the old General Register and abolished the Particular Register. It then introduced a new General Register of Sasines with separate divisions for each county register. This system still exists and the Register of Sasines now referred to is that established in 1868.

Very recently the Land Registration (Scotland) Act 1979 became law. It enables the registration of (say) B, as having a title to land rather than the registration of a deed granted by A to B. The register is however called the Land Register for Scotland and the new system is to come into force in stages at different times and in different areas at different times. The first stage began in 1981 in the county of Renfrew.

Rei interitus.—Even if the performance of an obligation has become impossible through no fault of the person charged with the obligation, that person is not freed from the duty to perform it except in very special circumstances. The clearest case in which performance is not enforced is perhaps that of *rei interitus*, namely, physical destruction of the property or subjects to which the contract relates.

Rei interventus.—*Rei interventus* is one of the principles embraced within the general doctrine of **personal bar** (*q.v.*). The doctrine is normally invoked to prevent a party resiling (withdrawing) from a contract which requires to be, but has not been, constituted by a probative writing. Such a party may not resile if he has by his words or conduct induced the other party to act on the faith of the contract as if it were perfectly constituted. (See also **Homologation.**)

Reinstatement.—This is the alternative to **re-engagement** (*q.v.*) where the tribunal finds that the employee has been unfairly dismissed. (See s. 69 of the Employment Protection (Consolidation) Act 1978.) Reinstatement means restoring the employee to the job from which he was dismissed as though the dismissal had never occurred. If the tribunal make an order for reinstatement they must state:

(a) how much the employer is to pay the employee for the loss of any benefit which he might have reasonably expected to receive if he had not been dismissed, including arrears of pay for the period between the end of his employment and the date set for his reinstatement;

(b) any rights and privileges, including seniority and pension rights, which must be restored to the employee; and

(c) the date by which the tribunal's order must be complied with.

The order will require the employee to be treated on reinstatement as if he had benefited (from the date on which he could have done so had he not been dismissed) from any improvement in the conditions of his employment. As reinstatement is more valuable than re-engagement the tribunal must first consider whether the employee can be reinstated. (See also **Re-engagement**.)

Relict.—The dictionary meaning of this word is "what is left behind after loss or decay of the rest". In Scots law it is used to designate the widow after her husband, or the widower after his wife, has died. The explanatory material under the heading **Legal rights** should be read. In the plural the word has the more general meaning of all the surviving members of a family after the death of the father and husband or mother and wife.

Remand.—Where a person who has been taken into custody by the police appears before a sheriff at the first or pleading diet and pleads not guilty he may either be released on bail or, if the crime in issue is a serious one or the accused person is of ill-repute, he may be remanded in custody to enable further inquiries to be made.

Removing.—See **Ejection** and **Removing**.

Reparation.—Broadly this word means to make amends or to pay compensation. In Scots law it has a similar meaning. If a person suffers injury, harm or loss to his person or property as a consequence of the fault of another he is entitled in law to have the injury or loss made good or compensated by the other. Most frequently, as, for instance, in the case of injury suffered by a person in a traffic accident, reparation takes the form of a money payment (usually referred to as damages) covering the cost of hospital treatment, replacement of goods destroyed, compensation for injury, and **solatium** (*q.v.*) for pain and suffering. If the vehicle in which the person concerned is travelling is damaged it will be repaired at the other's cost. Another common ground for which damages are sought is breach of contract. But the circumstances in which a person may seek reparation are numerous.

Reporter.—The word is used most frequently in relation to the person appointed by every regional and islands council under s. 36 of the Social Work (Scotland) Act 1968 for the purpose of arranging **children's hearings** (*q.v.*) and the other functions given to him under Part III of that Act. He must have the qualifications laid down in regulations made by the Secretary of State. Such a reporter cannot undertake any other official duties, but may conduct proceedings in children's cases which are required by the Act to come before a sheriff.

The term reporter is applied, sometimes rather loosely, to a person who is appointed under other statutes (*e.g.* the Town and Country Planning Acts and other Acts giving government departments and other official bodies powers to acquire land compulsorily) to hold any inquiry or a hearing into objections to ministerial proposals or a ministerial decision or an appeal against such proposals or decision and to report to the minister concerned.

Res gestae.—The literal meaning of this phrase is "the things done" or "the circumstances": the material facts of a case as opposed to mere hearsay. The phrase is generally used in reference to that which is apparently hearsay but is so immediately relevant to the matter in question that proof of it is permitted.

Res ipsa loquitur.—In court actions for damages for loss, harm or injury caused by negligence, certain presumptions or inferences of fact are accepted as shifting the onus of proof from the pursuer (who is bound in the first place to prove his case) to the defender.

The Latin maxim *res ipsa loquitur* is a loose rendering of the circumstances in which such a presumption can arise or an inference be drawn. The mere occurrence of an accident cannot give rise to such an inference and thus cannot place the onus of disproving negligence on the defender. Because its effect has been misunderstood the courts have from time to time thought it necessary to limit the application of the expression to certain classes of case. One such case is where the thing which causes the accident is within the exclusive control of the defender and his servants and would not have caused harm if proper control or proper care had been exercised unless it (the cause of the accident) can be explained as being consistent with due precautions having been taken.

Res judicata.—This Latin phrase embodies a doctrine having as its aim the limitation of litigation. A ground of action, heard and determined by a competent court, if rejected, cannot be founded on again provided the subject-matter in the second and earlier action is the same and the actions are founded on the same grounds of claim. The specific point raised in the second has been directly raised and concluded by the judgment in the first.

Reset or **Reset of theft.**—"Reset is the retention of goods obtained by theft, robbery, fraud, or embezzlement with the intention of keeping them from their true owner. The goods must have been obtained from the owner by someone other than the resetter (*i.e.* the person who retains possession of them) and have been obtained by the resetter with the consent of the person from whom he received them". (Excerpted from Sheriff G. H. Gordon's *Criminal Law*). The most common type of reset is the receiving by one person from another of goods which the other has stolen from the true owner and which the former knows to have been stolen. He may have got the goods innocently but if he becomes aware that the goods were stolen he becomes a resetter.

Residue (sometimes **Residue estate**).—The residue is what is left over. The law of succession uses it to describe that part of the estate (both heritable and moveable) of a person who leaves a will which remains after all debts, deathbed and funeral expenses, death duties, the legal and prior rights of the widow or widower and children in the estate and specific legacies bequeathed by the deceased have been met. The person to whom the residue is bequeathed is called the residuary legatee. The residue is necessarily an indefinite and uncertain sum until the amount of the whole estate is ascertained after death; the residuary legatee then being entitled to everything remaining after all these other payments and bequests have been met. There is no "residue" where no will exists, the deceased's estate being then disposed of in accordance with the rules of intestate succession.

Res perit.—This means no more than there is always a risk that goods contracted to be bought or sold may be lost or destroyed and *res perit domino* means that the risk of loss, deterioration or destruction of goods which are the subject of a contract rests on the owner of the goods. The owner may be either the seller or the purchaser, depending on whether ownership has passed from the one to the other.

Respondent.—This word is used to describe the defender in an appeal in a civil case. The appeal may be by way of an appeal to a higher court or by way of a stated case from say, a tribunal. The respondent may have been either the pursuer or the defender in the original action, depending on which of the two makes the appeal.

Restitution.—In many circumstances the law confers on a person a right to recover from some other person money or goods which that other person has no (or has no longer any) title to retain and to require that other person to repair or restore the money or goods to the former. The justification for this rule is natural justice and equity, so that no obligation will arise where an order to make restitution would be contrary to justice and equity, as where a payment morally due but not legally exigible has been made. Such a case is that where goods have been delivered to a person in error, or have been stolen by somebody or where a temporary title to possess money or goods has terminated. An action in court for recovery is competent and damages may be claimed if the money or goods are not repaired or restored. A second similar right exists where money is paid in the mistaken belief, for instance, that it is due or where as the result of an error of fact. An action in court similar to that above-mentioned is available in those cases also. A third type of case is where one party has lost and another gained without there being any intention to benefit the latter. A claim also exists in this case for an amount equal to the sum by which the other is enriched.

Retention.—Retention is the withholding by one party to a contract of due performance of his part of the contract in order to compel the other party to the contract duly to perform his part.

Retrocession.—A word infrequently used. It means the reconveyance to the former owner of a right which he has conveyed to another.

Return day.—The return day is prescribed by the rules of procedure which apply the summary cause introduced by the Sheriff Courts (Scotland) Act 1971. The summary cause replaced the earlier small debt court action and certain of the pre-1971 ordinary actions for sums of money not exceeding £500. It is a date entered by the sheriff clerk on the summons initiating the cause after the summons has been lodged by the pursuer in court. The summons is then returned to the pursuer or his solicitor and a copy is served on the defender. The summons will, at the same time, also bear a date seven days later than the return day on which the case will be first called in court. Rules 51

G

to 53 of the Act of Sederunt (Summary Cause Rules, Sheriff Court) 1976 set out the importance of the return day. The defender must before that date occurs, give notice to the sheriff clerk of his intention to defend the action should he intend to do so, specifying the grounds of defence. If the defender takes no action decree will be given against him. The pursuer should, of course, ascertain before the return day what steps, if any, the defender has taken.

Reversionary interest (or **right**).—Where a person conveys heritable property, or assigns incorporeal moveable property, to another in security he retains a right of reversion in the property. Another instance of a person having a reversionary right is where property is bequeathed to him in fee but some other person enjoys a liferent of it. So long as the liferent subsists the fiar has only a reversionary interest in the liferented property.

Right-of-way.—A public right-of-way is a right exercisable by any member of the public to pass from one public place to another by a recognised route. It is distinct from a servitude right-of-way and from a personal privilege of access. It may be created by grant but is normally established and acquired by prescriptive use (20 years) openly and without interruption in a manner implying a public right. It may be vindicated by any member of the public or by a society formed for the purpose. It will be lost by disuse for the prescriptive period (20 years) or by unchallenged contrary actings of the owner of the affected land, or may be extinguished by statute. (See **Prescription; Servitude.**)

Roup and sale.—See **Public Roup.**

Royal Assent.—Any statute starts life as a Bill presented to Parliament by one of Her Majesty's ministers or by a Member of Parliament who has been successful in the ballot for the right to present Bills which is held at the beginning of each session of Parliament. Thereafter the Bill goes through a number of stages in Parliament but even if and when it has survived first, second and third readings, Committee and Report Stages, etc., in both Houses of Parliament it does not become law. To become a statute it has to obtain the Royal Assent — that is, it has to be approved by the Sovereign, the procedure for which is to be found in the Royal Assent Act 1967.

Rubric.—In the case of a statute, the rubric includes the title and side notes. In the case of the official report of a court case, it means the headnotes.

S

Sale C.I.F. (Cost, Insurance, Freight).—Such a sale is one in which the price includes the cost not only of the goods sold but also of their insurance in transit and freight (cost of transportation). The seller has the duty in such a contract of making arrangements for the transportation of the goods to the destination contracted for and their delivery there, to ensure that the goods are insured for the buyer, to deliver the goods on board ship, rail, aeroplane or other vehicle and to forward the bill of lading, the insurance policy and invoice to the buyer. The goods become the buyer's when these documents are delivered to him and it then becomes his duty to pay the price.

Sale F.O.B. (Free on Board).—Such a sale is one in which the seller undertakes at his own expense to deliver the goods on board ship at an agreed port (or on some other kind of vehicle at an agreed place) for transportation to the buyer. The expense of the carriage and insurance falls on the buyer. Sale F.O.R. (Free on Rail) is similar for inland transport. The property in the goods transfers to the buyer when loaded on the ship or other vehicle and the price is then payable. The seller must give adequate notice to the buyer to enable him to insure the goods during transit. The price covers expenses up to and including delivery on board, rail, plane or other vehicle.

Sasine.—Giving sasine was the act of conferring legal possession of feudal property on a person (a purchaser, an heir) entitled to it. It also means infeftment by registration in the Register of Sasines of the deed transferring ownership. With changes in land and conveyancing law, sasine is little more than a generality.

Scottish Office.—This name has no legal standing. It is used to describe all the departments of government which are under the control of the Secretary of State for Scotland and which perform the functions which have been imposed or conferred on him by statute, common law and custom. (The Reorganisation of Offices (Scotland) Act 1937 may be referred to. Powers conferred by it to alter the administrative organisation of the Scottish departments have been used frequently since 1937.)

Search or (more fully) **Search for incumbrances.**—This is a record made by a professional searcher of all entries in relevant public registers relating to a particular area of heritable property (land, buildings, etc.) and to the successive owners of the property. The search must be made in the division of the General Register of Sasines which covers the area in which the property is situated and in the Register of Inhibitions and Adjudications. The search in the former will reveal, when the property is being sold, *prima facie* if the seller has a good title to the property and if there are any undischarged bonds (mortgages) or other burdens affecting it. The search in the latter will reveal whether or not there are any legal bars which prevent the seller disposing of the property. It does not go into such detail as to reveal liability for feuduty or other real burdens, building conditions or restrictions, servitudes or leases and other detailed matters affecting the property. The seller of the property must deliver an up-to-date search if the purchaser so requires and, in most cases, an interim search also (see also **Burden**).

Secured creditor.—A creditor who holds some special security for his debt, such as a floating charge or lien.

Sequestration.—Sequestration is a process by which the whole property of a bankrupt person is ingathered by, and set aside in the hands of, a neutral trustee for the use and division amongst the creditors of the bankrupt; the division being made in the shares to which the creditors are legally entitled. Sequestration for rent is a process of a different kind. It is a method by which a landlord to whom his tenant owes rent enforces his right to **hypothec** (*q.v.*). The right of hypothec confers on the landlord in the case of houses, shops and certain other premises a right of security, without the need to take possession, over such goods as furniture and furnishings, stock-in-trade and equipment and moveables generally but not over money, bonds, bills, the tenant's clothes, and, probably, his tools of trade. The enforcement of the right is effected by the landlord on being authorised by warrant of the court to sell the goods. The Bankruptcy (Scotland) Act 1913, s. 175 as amended by s. 12 of the Law Reform (Miscellaneous Provisions) (Scotland) Act 1980, deals with petitions for sequestration. (See **Bankruptcy.**)

Service.—This word has a number of meanings, some legal, some lay. Before the Succession (Scotland) Act 1964 was passed it was best known from the legal point of view in the context of succession to heritable property, but it is now of no importance in this context.

The word service is also important in the field of employment. A contract entered into between an employer and an employee is for hiring of service. Under it the servant lets out his services to the master or employer for reward or benefit, the employer being entitled to control the servant's work. (See **Contract of Employment.** The following are points not mentioned under that heading.)

A contract *of* service is not to be confused with a contract of agency or a contract *for* services. In the latter case the contractor is employed to achieve a result (*e.g.* paint a portrait) in his own way, the employer relying on the contractor's own skill to perform the contract and not exercising control in detail. The test of control is not however complete, because employees who theoretically, might be controlled or directed are not so. The employer, in many instances, does not have opportunity, or is unable through lack of knowledge, to exercise control. Other factors are the selection of the employee, the manner of remuneration and whether, in the case of a large organisation, he is a member of the organisation or of the organisation of a contractor performing work for the organisation. Civil servants are not employed under contracts of service. Unless the status of the person employed is quite clear, legal advice should be sought.

The sending or making available of documents by one party to the other party or parties to an action is also termed service (see **Action; Case**).

The word is also used in the context of feudal tenure of land, participation in warfare, religious worship, and it describes public services such as transport, water supply, roads and streets.

Servient Tenement.—See **Dominant tenement.**

Servitude.—A servitude is an accessory right that benefits one area of land and burdens another in different ownership. The two areas of land are usually, though not necessarily, contiguous. The benefited land is known as "the dominant tenement" and the burdened land as "the servient tenement". The right is exercisable by the owner of the dominant tenement and is suffered by the owner of the servient tenement, for instance where the owner of the dominant tenement has a right of access to his property over the servient tenement. It may be natural, as for instance where the servient tenement is at a lower level and water from the dominant runs without human design over it; or it may be legal, where for instance a conveyance or a private Act of Parliament confers a right on the owner of certain land to take a water supply from other land. More frequently, however, it is conventional, that is, created by agreement or contract. Servitudes are classed as urban if they affect buildings, rural if they affect open ground, and positive where they enable rights of use to be exercised *e.g.* by prohibiting the erection of buildings or of buildings above a certain height, and negative where they limit the use to which the servient tenement can be put. Rights of golfing, curling, or skating, walking, fishing, shooting, are not servitudes; they are privileges having the force of personal licences only.

Sheriff.—The word sheriff is used in a general way to describe any person who acts as a judge in the sheriff court. Strictly until 1971, however, it meant any one of the sheriffs who was the senior judge in any of the 12 sheriffdoms in Scotland. Since 1971 the senior judge in the sheriffdom is the **sheriff principal** (q.v.) and sheriff is the word used in relation to any of the 70 sheriffs who hear and decide the day-to-day civil and criminal cases in the sheriff courts thoughout Scotland from Lerwick in the north to Stranraer in the south. The largest number in any court is in the sheriff court of the sheriffdom of Glasgow and Strathkelvin, situated in Glasgow where there are 20 full-time sheriffs. There are four further full-time sheriffs (colloquially referred to as "floating sheriffs") who move from one court to another as work demands. Additionally there are "temporary" sheriffs not full-time, who spend short periods (a day or two) in any court in which there is an urgent need for a sheriff perhaps because the resident sheriff is unwell or because there is a sudden expansion of work.

Five or six centuries ago the sheriff was an administrator and collector of taxes, fines and other sums due to the Crown. Nowadays his functions are predominantly judicial although he has some administrative functions also. Before appointment he must have engaged in legal practice for at least ten years if a **solicitor,** five years if he is an **advocate.** He exercises a very wide civil and criminal jurisdiction.

He has, however, to remit to the Court of Session any civil case which is outwith his jurisdiction or raises a particularly difficult question of law. In criminal cases the more serious crimes (*e.g.* murder) are tried by the High Court of Justiciary, not by the sheriff and he has power to remit to that court criminal cases where for instance he takes the view that he has no power to impose a severe enough penalty on the guilty person. His judgments in civil cases can be appealed to the sheriff principal or directly to the Inner House of the Court of Session. The sheriff relies on the **sheriff clerk** to do the executive work associated with the court.

Sheriff clerk.—The sheriff clerk is the clerk of the sheriff court. His powers and duties are to act as clerk in every matter in which a sheriff has jurisdiction and his functions are therefore very wide, including not only the organisation of the work of the court but also assisting the sheriff in court, keeping records of cases dealt with, the granting of confirmations and other matters connected with commissary affairs. In addition to having these court functions he also has administrative functions such as acting as auditor in the taxation of the accounts of solicitors in court proceedings and commissary affairs. The sheriff clerk is appointed by the Secretary of State. Every sheriff court has a sheriff clerk and, except in the smallest courts, he has a depute or deputes and clerical and other ancillary staff to assist him. There are now only one or two sheriff clerks who are part-time officials; at one time most were part-time.

Sheriff officer.—A sheriff officer is an officer of the sheriff court in the sheriffdom for which he is appointed by the sheriff principal. His principal functions are connected with the doing of **diligence.** On instructions from the pursuer or the pursuer's solicitor he takes the initial procedural steps in the raising of an **action,** the enforcement of a decree given by the sheriff (*e.g.* by **arrestment** of wages or goods or by **poinding**) and the taking of steps required to ensure the attendance of witnesses. It is also he who takes the procedural steps necessary to enable **warrant sales** to take place as well as other sales of poinded or arrested goods. Most sheriff officers are also **messengers-at-arms,** and perform the functions of the latter where no messenger is available. A list of sheriff officers and the sheriffdoms in which they act will be found in the *Scottish Law Directory* and the *Parliament House Book.*

Sheriff principal.—The office of sheriff principal was created by the Sheriff Courts (Scotland) Act 1971. Prior to 27 July 1971 (when that Act came into operation) the office was known as that of sheriff and each sheriff was the senior judge in the sheriffdom to which he was appointed. There were then 12 sheriffdoms and, but for the Sheriff of Edinburgh and Peebles and the Sheriff of Glasgow, all of the sheriffs were part-time, carrying on practice as senior counsel in the courts. Section 6 of the Law Reform (Miscellaneous Provisions) (Scotland) Act 1980 empowers the Secretary of State to authorise the sheriff principal of one sheriffdom to act in another.

On 1 January 1975 the number of sheriffdoms was reduced to six and a sheriff principal was appointed for each by the Crown on the recommendation of the Secretary of State. The office of sheriff principal then became full-time. The right of appeal to him from the judgment of a sheriff remains but as such an appeal can be made direct to the Court of Session there are relatively few appeals to the sheriffs principal.

A large number of administrative duties have been added to the sheriff principal's functions by ss. 15 to 17 of the 1971 Act and by administrative arrangements made with the Scottish Courts Administration (a department responsible to both the Secretary of State and the Lord Advocate for some of their respective functions). Each sheriff principal for instance, now has responsibility for ensuring the speedy and efficient disposal of business in the courts in his sheriffdom, the making of arrangements for the duties and leave of the sheriffs in his sheriffdom and for fixing sittings and the business of these courts and the sessions therein for civil business.

Signet.—In full this expression is "The King's Signet", and refers to the Seal of the Court of Session with which are sealed "whatever passes by the warrant of the Session" (see Erskine's *Principles*), including summonses and diligence. An **action** cannot be begun in the Court of Session until the summons has been signeted.

Sine die.—This means without fixed date, *i.e.* indefinitely.

Sine qua non.—Used to describe something (a document, an entry in court records, a payment) which must be done to enable some further action or further step to be taken.

Si petitur tantum.—If, *e.g.* a payment is required to be made only if the person entitled to it asks for it to be made, this Latin phrase can be used to describe it. Shortly, it means "Only so far as demanded".

Sist.—This term occurs in connection with court procedure, and broadly speaking, means the suspension of that procedure in a particular action for particular purposes. It is a principle of Scots law that litigation should be conducted in accordance with the rules and regulations laid down by statute or Act of Sederunt or accepted by settled practice and that the court should give judgment on as early a date as possible. Circumstances may emerge in which the court will allow the prescribed procedure to be suspended *i.e.* sisted. This will be done only if there are strong grounds for doing so. Examples of such grounds are: to enable a party to an action to complete his title to heritage or moveables, to allow a judicial factor to be appointed, to enable a party to an action to apply for legal aid or to await the result of another impending action or an arbitration which is likely to have an effect in the sisted proceedings. A sist suspends proceedings for a definite period or until the occurrence of a particular event, and it may be extended or recalled. All these steps are taken by the court on representations made to it by any one of the parties concerned.

Solatium.—The word has two main aspects. In cases of personal injury the injured person is, if the injury was caused as the result of the fault (act or omission) of another, entitled to receive from the other, a sum in name of solatium for: (a) pain and suffering occasioned by the injury inflicted on him or her; (b) loss of faculties and amenities; and (c) loss of expectation of life. These three elements do not represent the injured person's financial loss. In cases such as assault, defamation, malicious prosecution and the like, the whole award is in the nature of solatium and must be assessed by regard to the nature and extent of the dishonour done, the injury to feeling and reputation and the whole circumstances. (See **Reparation.**)

Until the Damages (Scotland) Act 1976 came into operation the word also signified a different ground of solatium. This ground was intended as recompense for the grief and suffering caused to certain of the relatives of a person who died as the result of some other person's fault. Under the new law (*i.e.* since 1976) a relative (defined in s. 1 (1) of and Schedule 1 to the Act) may claim instead a loss of society award. It is not given the name of solatium by the Act and is designed to compensate the relative for the loss of the non-patrimonial (*i.e.* non-financial) benefit which he or she might have been expected to derive from the injured person's society and guidance had he or she not died. Neither a claim for solatium nor one for loss of society transmits to the claimant's executor.

Solemn procedure.—This is the procedure in the criminal courts in accordance with which a person charged on **indictment** with the commission of a crime or offence is tried. Cases before the **High Court of Justiciary** always proceed on indictment. Amongst other specialities a trial in which solemn procedure is followed may be before a judge of the High Court (judges of the High Court are also judges of the Court of Session) or before a sheriff and, in either case, before a jury of 15 persons. Solemn procedure is contrasted with summary procedure when the judge or the sheriff sits without a jury.

Solicitors.—Solicitors are members of the legal profession. The public generally tend to apply the description "lawyer" to a solicitor rather than to other members of the profession. In Scotland there are about 3,500 solicitors in practice, some on their own account, others as members of or assistants to legal firms, legal advisers or executives to central or local government, industrial or commercial bodies. The work they do is so very varied that specialisation amongst them is, though attempted, uncommon, except where a large number of solicitors work in co-ordination. Most solicitors in private practice rely on *conveyancing* (the purchase and sale of houses, buildings and land and preparation of the necessary deeds of transfer) for the work which provides them with a livelihood but there are many other fields as, for instance, **reparation, wills** and **succession,** actions in the Court of Session, sheriff and district courts. Every practising solicitor in Scotland must be a member of the Law Society of Scotland and hold both a practising certificate and a professional indemnity insurance policy in a scheme organised by the society, and contribute to the guarantee fund (required by statute to be maintained by the society) by means of which the profession at large ensures that members of the public are safeguarded against misuse of their funds, or errors made, by solicitors. The Court of Session actually admits solicitors to the profession and this is symbolic of the fact that all lawyers are responsible primarily to the court for their professional behaviour. A solicitor may be struck off the roll for malpractice or misconduct; the Scottish Solicitors Discipline Tribunal take the initial steps in such cases.

There are a number of groups of solicitors known by special names, as for instance Writers to the Signet (W.S. for short), most of whom are located in Edinburgh and whose special significance in modern times is that they as a society have premises and a library of their own and provide pensions for widows of deceased members. Solicitors of the Supreme Courts (S.S.C.) are a similar body. In Aberdeen there is a Society of Advocates to which the local solicitors belong and there are faculties of solicitors and procurators in many localities.

Solicitor-General for Scotland.—The Solicitor-General for Scotland is not to be confused with the English law office having the title of Solicitor-General. He is an experienced advocate (usually in practice when appointed) and is the junior of the two law officers of the Crown in Scotland. He is appointed by the Prime Minister and has all the powers of the Lord Advocate in criminal matters and most of the work arising out of prosecutions which require to be dealt with at ministerial level is in practice dealt with by him. He also assists the Lord Advocate with other functions including duties in the Court of Session and the giving of legal advice to the government and its departments. In the absence of the Lord Advocate he has authority to perform these functions. The Solicitor-General does not resign when the Lord Advocate resigns (if the latter for instance is made a judge) but it is usual for him to succeed the Lord Advocate in his office. Like the Lord Advocate he demits office when the government of which he is a member ceases to hold office.

Solum.—The *solum* is an area of ground. The word is most frequently used in relation to the ground upon which buildings or other edifices have been constructed. The owner of the building also owns the *solum* though he may not own the minerals beneath. If the building be a flatted **tenement** the owners of all the flats have a common interest in the *solum* to ensure support for their flats, but the *solum* is owned by the owner of the ground floor flat so far as it lies beneath the flat he owns.

Special defence.—There are certain special defences which a person accused of a crime is not permitted to rely on unless a plea of special defence is tendered and recorded at the first **diet** and not less than ten clear days before the trial diet. There is no authoritative list of special defences but it has been said that the categories of special defences now recognised cannot be extended. In order to be relevant the special defence must set out facts which, if proved, would lead to his acquittal. The following are the recognised categories of special defences: alibi, insanity, incrimination (impeachment), self-defence and, though less certainly, that the accused was asleep at the time when he committed the crime (involuntary dissociation). Intoxication is not a defence although when involuntary it will have the effect of reducing the quality of the offence. Neither diminished responsibility nor provocation nor any other plea in mitigation is a special defence and will not therefore exculpate the accused.

Specific implement.—It is a general rule of Scots law that a person who has entered into a contract for the performance, for example, of some work or the delivery of specific goods may obtain a decree from the court requiring the person who has undertaken to do the work or deliver the goods to implement what he has undertaken to do. Such a decree is called a decree *ad factum praestandum* and if the defender wilfully fails to implement it he may in the end suffer imprisonment. The court has discretion whether to order specific implement or not and, in some circumstances, decree will not be granted. It will not be, for instance, where the obligation is to pay money (imprisonment for civil debt is not possible except in the case of failure to pay **aliment** due under a decree), where performance is impossible or where decree would cause exceptional hardship. But decree will be granted, for instance, where the contract is to sell a specific thing or a specific area of land, to build a house, to put a tenant in possession of subjects let, to enter into and remain in such subjects and to furnish and heat a shop. Where a defender refuses to implement a contract signing and delivering a deed, *e.g.* a disposition of a house, the court can authorise someone else to sign it. The pursuer may, as an alternative, sue for damages.

Stamp duty.—Many payments of dues made to the courts (*e.g.* on the signeting of a summons) or payments of duty to the Inland Revenue (*e.g.* on a conveyance) were formerly made by affixing Revenue stamps of the required value to the document; hence the title "stamp duty". The Stamp Act 1891 and the Stamp Duties Management Act of the same year deal with most payments which had to be so made but the Conveyancing (Scotland) Act 1874 and other Acts deal with the stamp duty on particular deeds. These Acts have been substantially amended by legislation over the years, and in many instances stamps are no longer used for the purpose mentioned above. Deeds conveying land which are required to bear duty, bear impressed stamps and fees payable to courts and the Keeper of the Registers are paid in cash. The *Parliament House Book,* and the *Scottish Law Directory* contain tables of the duties payable in most circumstances.

Standard security.—The Conveyancing and Feudal Reform (Scotland) Act 1970 introduced the "standard security" as a new method by which a borrower of money may give the lender security for it over land or an interest in land which he owns. It may be security for a fixed or fluctuating sum and is not necessarily for a maximum amount. Since the passing of the Act it is the only competent means of granting such security. The security must be in one or other of two forms set out in Schedule 2 to the Act. The first imposes a personal obligation on the borrower to repay the sum borrowed, and the second is used where the personal obligation is created by a separate deed. A standard security is regulated by the standard conditions set out in Schedule 3 to the Act, but these conditions may be varied by agreement except condition 11 and the provisions relating to the **powers of sale and foreclosure**. A standard security does not become effective until it has been recorded in the **Register of Sasines** (*q.v.*). The Act also contains provisions about the assignation, restriction, discharge, and redemption of the security, the repayment of the sum borrowed and the sale of the security subjects by the lender in default of repayment by the borrower.

Stated case.—One of the means by which an appeal may be made from the decision of a lower court or tribunal to the Court of Session is the stated case. Such an appeal is on a question of law (in some rare cases statutes provide for appeal on fact): and the appellant is required to state what question of law he wishes to be placed before the appeal court. The sheriff or tribunal by which the decision has been given prepares a draft stated case which consists of a statement of the facts and concludes with the question of law to be answered. The draft is thereafter adjusted between the sheriff or tribunal and the parties, with the former having the deciding role. An appeal in a criminal case follows the same procedure.

Status.—The legal meaning of this word is the legal standing or position of a person. The law confers capacities, liabilities or incapacities on certain groups of persons and whether a person belongs to a particular group or not is for the most part determined by force of law alone, the person himself having little control over the matter. But if a person gets married his or her status is altered because he or she assumes different capacities and liabilities and whether he or she gets married or not is a matter for himself or herself to decide. Status is however, more than, and different from, a mere voluntary relationship between one person and another; it involves a general condition or standing in legal matters which determines the individual's powers, etc. The question of status is a difficult one.

Status quo.—Means the state in which a thing or a situation already is and **status quo ante** means the state in which any situation, fact or other thing was before a certain date, event, legal action or any other matter effected an alteration in that state.

Statute.—This is an Act of Parliament. Some statutes are very old but still in operation. Acts of the Parliament of Scotland passed before the Union of the Parliaments in 1707 are the oldest that apply to Scotland, but Acts passed by Parliament at Westminster are far more numerous and important. The word is synonymous with legislation and is sometimes used as applying not to the whole of an Act but only to some part of, or provision in, an Act. Where legislation of any kind is in force in relation to any subject, it is authoritative in that it overrules any rule of law inconsistent with it and allows no option to its implementation unless it clearly appears to be permissive only.

Statutory instrument.—This is a document consisting of rules, regulations or orders made in exercise of powers conferred by Parliament on a government department or other body or persons (including the Court of Session and High Court of Justiciary). Every such instrument falls into the category of **subordinate legislation**. The most important instruments are orders in council, departmental rules, regulations or orders, **Acts of Sederunt** and **Acts of Adjournal.** Most are presented to Parliament, some for approval before being made, others for possible disapproval after being made. They may be challenged on the grounds of *vires*, that is, on the ground that they (or some part of them) are outwith the scope of the powers which Parliament has conferred on the authority making them. (See the Statutory Instruments Act 1946.)

Statutory small tenancy.—This is a form of tenancy of an agricultural holding to which the Crofters Acts (see **Croft**) apply by virtue of the Small Landholders (Scotland) Acts 1886 to 1931. These Acts should be consulted but, as in the case of crofts, the statutory and other provisions must be looked at with the basic law of agricultural holdings in mind.

Stipendiary magistrate.—Power is conferred by s. 5 of the District Courts (Scotland) Act 1975 on local authority district councils to appoint a stipendiary magistrate to deal with cases in the **district court**. Glasgow District Council alone has so far made use of that power, thus following Glasgow Corporation who had made use of a similar provision in earlier legislation. Where no such magistrate is appointed, justices, who do not require to be legally qualified, act as judges in the district court.

Stoppage in transitu.—The seller of goods who has not been paid for them and who learns before the buyer or his agent has taken delivery of them from the carrier (by land or water — there seems to be no authority about air) or other person entrusted with transmission of them to the buyer, that the buyer has become insolvent, may resume possession of the goods and retain them until payment of the price is made or offered. This procedure is termed *stoppage in transitu.* Stoppage is effected by taking actual possession of the goods or by giving notice of the seller's claim to the carrier or other person in time to prevent delivery to the buyer. The seller does not on recovering possession of the goods recover the ownership of them. If the buyer fails to make or tender payment after stoppage the seller is entitled to re-sell the goods if they are perishable or if he has given notice to the buyer of his intention to re-sell and the buyer does not within a reasonable time pay or tender the price.

Subjects.—This is a very general term used to refer to property, more commonly **heritage** though also **moveables** in some contexts, which is being referred to in any written document, *e.g.* a deed, writ, summons or letter.

Sub judice.—When a matter is *sub judice*, it is before the courts for decision of the whole or part of the matters in dispute. In such circumstances the matter cannot be looked at or referred to formally in any other legal proceedings, or commented on publicly or in the press or other sources of news transmission nowadays usually referred to as the "media".

Subordinate legislation.—These words cover all **statutory instruments** and other rules (*e.g.* **bye-laws**) made in exercise of statutory powers. The provisions in them are read along with the **statute** under which they are made, and when such a statute is repealed, all statutory instruments so made are impliedly repealed also unless expressly saved.

Subrogation.—Literally the word subrogation means substituition. An instance of its use in law is where an insurer has indemnified the insured person against loss for which another party is legally liable. The insurer is, without any formal assignation, subrogated to the insured's right to recover from the person legally liable and may raise an action against the latter in name of the person he has insured. Alternatively the insurer is entitled to the benefit of compensation recovered by the insured person from the person legally liable to make good the loss.

Succession.—The rules of succession regulate the way in which property is, on the death of the owner of it, handed over to those who succeed to it in his place. Universal succession deals with the disposal of the whole estate and assets of the deceased as distinct from singular succession which is succession to particular items or property transferred to a successor during the life of the deceased as on gift of sale. The law of succession can be said to have three main aspects. The first deals with the rights which are conferred by the law on certain survivors independently of the wishes of the deceased; the second with **intestate** succession where the deceased leaves no will or other document directing how his estate is to be disposed of; and the third with the case where the deceased leaves such a will or document, and is referred to as **testate** succession. Heritable and moveable property have to be considered separately. The powers and duties of **executors** and **trustees** can also be said to fall within the law of succession.

Sui juris.—Used to describe a person who is under no disability affecting his legal capacity to convey property, to enter a contract, to raise and pursue a court action or to defend an action raised against him. An **incapax** is in the opposite position.

Summary action.—The **Summary cause** has replaced the summary action.

Summary cause.—Until 1976 all actions in the sheriff courts, except small debt cases (*i.e.* actions for recovery of sums less than £50) were conducted in accordance with formal rules. Since 1971, however, an action in which the value of the property in dispute or the indebtedness or damages sued for does not exceed £500 is called a "summary cause". It is intended to provide a quick and easy way to settle disputes which it has not been possible to settle out of court. The action may be begun by the pursuer himself but there are forms, rules and time limits to be observed (see Act of Sederunt (Summary Cause Rules, Sheriff Court) 1976 as amended by Act of Sederunt (Summary Cause Rules Amendment Rules) 1978). (See **Return Day**.)

Summary conviction.—Means the conviction of a person accused in summary proceedings in a sheriff or district court and found to have committed an offence. The proceedings will have been conducted by way of summary complaint and not on indictment and thus, of course, without a jury. Section 8 of the Criminal Justice (Scotland) Act 1980 provides, however, for indictment in certain summary causes.

Summary warrant.—These words refer to one of the elements in the summary procedure made available to local authorities by s. 247 of the Local Government (Scotland) Act 1947 for the recovery of rates levied by them on persons by whom payment is due but who have not made payment. An authority's collector of rates may give to a person by whom rates are payable a notice requiring him to pay within 14 days the amount due by him. If at the end of that period the amount or any part of it is still unpaid the sheriff is required to grant a summary warrant for recovery thereof plus ten per cent. (No further procedure is required.) The amount thus due is to be recovered by **poinding,** sheriff officers being authorised by the warrant to effect the poinding and sell the goods poinded on three days' notice. A summary warrant also authorises arrestment of the debtor's funds. A similar procedure is available to the Collector of Taxes in respect of unpaid taxes. Section 63 of the Taxes Management Act 1970 should be consulted.

Summons.—A summons is a summoning or authoritative call to appear in court. The word is also used to describe generally the

H

document by which such a call is made, although the title of the document may be different (*e.g.* initial writ is the term employed in ordinary actions in the sheriff court). It is normally used in civil cases, proceeds in the name of the Sovereign, sets out the reason why the person to whom it is addressed is required to appear in court, the facts upon which the pursuer relies, and the remedies which the pursuer desires the court to make available to him.

Superior; Superiority.—See **Vassal**.

T

Tacit relocation.—This phrase is used most frequently in relation to leases, but it applies in other spheres of law also, *e.g.* partnerships. In the case of leases it signifies that if the stipulated duration of a lease expires without either party having given notice to the other of intent to terminate the lease, the parties are held to have renewed the lease for another year. If the lease is of an agricultural holding, s. 16 of the Agricultural Holdings (Scotland) Act 1947 enacts a provision similar in effect but, while in the case of other subjects tacit relocation does not operate if there is anything in the lease to rebut the presumption, in the case of the lease of an agricultural holding it applies by virtue of the statutory provision whether or not the lease contains such a provision.

Tack duty.—Tack is a Scottish term (little used in modern times) for a lease. The tack duty was the sum (rent) payable to the owner of the land by the tacksman (the tenant). (See **Lease**.)

Taxation of accounts.—The law makes provision for the fees and expenses charged by a solicitor for his work in conducting an action in court to be scrutinised or, as it is called "taxed" if the court so orders. In an action in the Court of Session, the auditor of the Court of Session, in an action in the sheriff court, the sheriff clerk or a solicitor appointed by the sheriff, will carry out the taxation. Although not referred to as taxation the auditor or the sheriff clerk will also audit accounts of charges made by solicitors to their clients for, as an example, winding up an executry. This may be done at the instance of beneficiaries, the executors or even the solicitor himself with the consent of the beneficiaries. The auditor or sheriff clerk charges a fee for such audits. (See **Auditor of Court**.)

Teinds.—Teinds or tithes are a one-tenth proportion of the produce of land and were originally used for the support and maintenance of the church and clergy. Since the Reformation in the 16th century they have not been used for that purpose but have become an interest in land subject to payment of a stipend for the maintenance of the clergy. They are owned by the person having a title to them (the "titular"). At the same time they are a burden on lands due by the owner of the land (the "heritor") who is liable to contribute to the upkeep of the parish church. The heritor pays to the titular the amount by way of teind for payment of which he is liable. This complicated structure arises out of the history of the relationship between Church and State and cannot be fully understood without much study.

Since the passing of the Church of Scotland (Property and Endowments) Act 1925 stipend has been payable only in money from the date (after 1925) when the benefice (*i.e.* ministry in a parish church) first became vacant. The last such ministry only recently became vacant. Stipends of small amounts have all been compulsorily redeemed. A teind roll for every parish is required to be made up and this for the most part has been done. The roll specifies the total teind of the parish, the amount applicable to each landowner who has a title to teinds, the value of the whole stipend payable to the minister and the proportion payable by each landowner. Once the teind roll of a parish has been finalised the values in it are binding. In effect teinds have been almost wholly exhausted by the stipend paid out of them.

Tendendas.—A word now seldom used. It refers to the clause in a deed relating to land which expresses the tenure on which the land is held.

Tender.—A tender is an offer of money or any other thing in satisfaction of a debt or other liability. An example is to be found in the context of an action for damages in court. If agreement as to the amount of damages cannot be reached, the defender, if he admits liability, may lodge a tender in court. If the pursuer accepts it, the case is finished; if he rejects it the case proceeds but should the court in the end award him a smaller amount by way of damages than the amount tendered he will obtain only the smaller amount. It is a matter of tactics at what point a tender should be made and what the amount of the tender should be.

A second meaning of the word is found in the expression "legal tender" which means coin or paper money which a creditor may be compelled to accept in satisfaction of his debt. He cannot, however, be compelled to accept for example, paper money or nickel for gold.

Tenement.—This is a general term used to refer to any heritable property, more commonly to heritable property which is or forms a block of flats (the earliest being in the Old Town of Edinburgh, it is said).

Tertium quid.—A third proposition or conclusion distinct in character and quality from two component parts or either of them.

Testamentary writing.—This expression is considered under the title **Will**. It is a generic, not a specific term. It is used to describe a deed, instrument or document of a testamentary nature. Any such instrument may bear one of a variety of names such as will, testament, last will and testament, trust disposition and settlement. In it the testator makes provision for the disposal of his means and estate after his death.

Testate.—If a person dies having made a **will** or other testamentary writing disposing of the property which he owns or of which he is in a position to dispose at the time of his death, he is said to have died testate and to be a "testator". His means and estate are thus disposed of in accordance with the provisions of his **testamentary writing** (*q.v.*), subject to the overriding right of his spouse and children to their legal rights. A person may omit to dispose of some part of his estate in which case he will have died intestate so far as that part is concerned (see **Intestate**). This subject is examined more fully under the title **Will**.

Testator.—See **testate**.

Testing clause.—The testing clause is the clause with which all deeds or writings in traditional form end. It is the attestation clause and sets out the fact of the signature (also called execution) of the deed by the granter and by the witnesses whom it names and designs. It also records the date and place of signature and may narrate any changes made in the deed (by erasure, say) before signature (see **Attestation**).

Third party.—In a civil action the pursuer or pursuers and the defender or defenders are the parties to the action. Another person who has an interest in the outcome of the action may be sisted (see **Sist**) as a party to the action at his own request. A person may also be sisted, where the action is before the Court of Session, at the request of one or other of the parties. If the action is before the sheriff court a person may be sisted at the request of the defender only. Any one of these person is termed a "third party" to the action.

Similarly, in the field of contract there are normally two contracting parties but another person not party to the contract may have an interest in the substance of the contract and is known as a third party to the contract. A familiar instance of the latter arises out of a motor insurance contract where a person who has no contractual relationship with either of the parties to the contract (the insurer or the insured) may yet make a claim against the insured for damages, any sum to which the third party is found entitled being paid by the insurer.

Thirlage.—See **Multures**.

Tholing an assize.—The word *thole* ("tholing" is a participle) has no special legal meaning, but where a person is charged with a crime he may put forward certain pleas in bar of trial, one of which is *res judicata*. This means that the accused person has already been charged with, and the court has decided, the issue involved; the accused is said then to have "tholed his assize". To support this plea it must be shown that the crime charged in the second indictment is the same as that charged in the first, and to be proved by the same evidence.

Time-bar.—The lapse of time may affect the legal rights of a party in many ways and may bar him from taking steps he could have taken earlier or from enforcing his rights. Very briefly, some of the circumstances in which time bars the taking of an action are:

(a) the parties to an agreement may themselves create a time-bar, for instance by limiting the time within which a guarantee will be available;

(b) statutory limitations (also referred to as short prescriptions) which render various kinds of obligations unenforceable after a certain time, *e.g.* an obligation to pay money due to a shop-keeper is extinguished after five years;

(c) statutory limitations on the time for bringing actions;

(d) the statutory prescription which wholly extinguishes rights or obligations after the lapse of 20 years;

(e) the statutory prescription, known as "positive prescription", by which a bad or doubtful title to land is established or fortified if certain conditions are satisfied and the land has been possessed openly, peaceably and without judicial interference for ten years (see **Prescription; Limitation of Actions**).

(f) the enforcement of a right in the usual fashion may be barred simply by the person to whom it belongs delaying to take action to enforce it. This is known as *mora*.

Totting-up.—This is not strictly a legal expression. Section 93 (3) of the Road Traffic Act 1972 provides that where a person who has been convicted of an offence involving obligatory or discretionary disqualification from driving has, within three years before he committed the offence, been convicted on two or more occasions of a similar offence and his driving licence has been endorsed on each occasion, the court shall, unless there are mitigating circumstances, order him to be disqualified from driving for not less than six months. The convictions are taken account of together, or, more colloquially, are totted up.

Treasure trove.—These words are applied to precious articles found concealed in the ground or in the fabric of a building, there being no proof of their ownership. Such articles belong to the Crown. Well-known instances of treasure trove are the collections of silverware found many years ago on Traprain Law, near East Linton, and more recently in 1958 on St Ninian's Isle in Shetland.

Trespass.—Trespass has a very limited meaning in Scotland. It is any temporary intrusion upon the land of another person without his permission or without legal justification. Under the Trespass (Scotland) Act 1865 and certain other special Acts, trespass is a crime. Damages are not recoverable for mere trespass but only if some actual damage is done or the landowner is assaulted or insulted. If there is ground for believing the trespass will be repeated or continued, the court may be asked to interdict the trespasser from returning to, or remaining on, the land.

Trial.—The hearing of a case in criminal proceedings is called a trial; so also is a proof in civil proceedings which takes place before a judge and jury or a judge sitting alone.

Tribunal.—In a general sense a tribunal is any court of justice or arbitration or other body appointed to adjudicate on some matter. In more recent times the word has been used most frequently to refer to any of the many tribunals established for adjudicating on disputes arising in particular fields of a statutory nature. They include local tribunals, the Lands Tribunal for Scotland, the National Insurance Commissioners, industrial tribunals, rent assessment committees, rent tribunals, supplementary benefit appeal tribunals and other tribunals concerned with matters arising out of public administration (*e.g.* out of the provisions of the Town and Country Planning (Scotland) Acts). These last are usually referred to as administrative tribunals.

The Tribunals and Inquiries Act 1971 set up the Council on Tribunals (of which there is a Scottish Committee) which keeps the work of many tribunals under review and provides for appeals from these tribunals to the Court of Session on questions of law.

Trust.—A trust has been defined by Erskine (see **Common**

Law) as "of the nature of disposition by which a proprietor transfers to another the property of the subject entrusted not that it should remain with him but that it may be applied for behoof of a third party". But a trust may arise by implication and a person may find himself a trustee with his agreement or even against his wishes. There is a major classification of trusts into private and public. In the former only individuals named or designated in the deed creating the trust can claim an interest or benefit; the latter are for the benefit of a section of the public and may be enforced by a public action (*popularis actio*) and continue for a substantial period of time or in perpetuity. In all these cases the trust is usually created by a trust deed which sets out the purposes of the trust, the beneficiaries and the trustees. The law of trusts is wide in scope and merits careful study. Much of it has its foundation in the common law but there is much also enacted in statutes, *e.g.* the Trusts (Scotland) Act 1921 and the Trusts (Scotland) Act 1961 as amended by ss. 8 and 13 of the Law Reform (Miscellaneous Provisions) (Scotland) Act 1980.

Trust deed for creditors.—An insolvent (bankrupt) person who grants a trust deed for his creditors conveys his whole estate to a trustee named in the deed for the benefit of his creditors. The trustee is the representative of the creditors, holds the estate for them and distributes it among them according to their various claims and preferences. The Bankruptcy Acts contain almost no provisions about trust deeds for creditors. (See **Bankruptcy.**)

Trustee.—A trustee is usually the same person as the executor of the estate of a deceased person but he is called a trustee because his functions are determined in many respects by the testator's will (if there is one) and are not simply to ingather and distribute the estate but also to retain and manage it, *e.g.* during the lifetime of a beneficiary to whom a liferent of the estate has been bequeathed by the will.

There are also trustees in many other types of case, *e.g.* a trustee under a **trust deed for creditors** granted by a business-man who cannot meet his debts. In all cases a trustee is a person who has the legal title to property but who holds it in trust for the benefit of others. (See **Trust; Trust deed for creditors; executor.**)

Tutor.—A tutor is a person who has the power and facility conferred on him (now mainly by statute though originally by the common law) to regulate the upbringing, the physical and intellectual welfare and education of a pupil child. He also has power to manage any property heritable or moveable belonging to the pupil.

A tutor is essential to a pupil, his natural tutor before the passing of the Guardianship Act 1973 being his father or, if the father was deceased, his mother. Since 1973 either parent can be the child's tutor, any disagreement between them being resolved by the court on application. In the case of an illegitimate pupil child the mother has always been, and still is, the natural tutor. If, in the case of a legitimate child, either parent dies, the other becomes sole tutor and if the surviving parent also dies a person nominated by either parent in his or her **will** becomes tutor. The position where one parent predeceases the other leaving a will in which a tutor is nominated appears to be that the nominee will act as tutor along with the survivor as joint tutor and that, after the death of the surviving parent, the nominee will be sole tutor, or, if the survivor also leaves a will nominating a tutor, the two nominees will act as joint tutors. (The Guardianship Acts are not however clear on the point.)

The court have an overriding power to appoint a factor *loco tutoris* (in place of a tutor) to supersede a parent as tutor (or guardian), or, if there be no tutor (natural, testamentary, or appointed by the court) or if neither parent is fit to act as tutor, the court on the application of any person may appoint a guardian who will take the place of the tutor (s. 4 (2A) of the Guardianship of Infants Act 1925) or commit the care of the child to a local authority (s. 11 of the 1973 Act).

A parent acting as tutor is deemed to be a trustee within the meaning of the Trusts (Scotland) Acts 1921 and 1961. The pupil may hold property but has no legal personality in this sphere, all legal powers being in the tutor. (See also **Guardian; Pupil; Minor; Custody; Tutor; Curator; Quadriennium utile.**)

U

Uberrimae fidei.—This Latin phrase is used in relation to certain contracts. A literal translation is "with the most perfect frankness". One of the best known fields in which it applies is insurance contracts. In entering into such a contract each party must disclose all the facts known, or which should have been known and which might be material to the undertaking of the risk or the premium to be charged. It is essential that there should be no misrepresentation or concealment of material facts. If there is, even if innocently done, the contract is **voidable.**

Udal land.—Udal land exists in Orkney and Shetland only. Most has now been feudalised but such as remains is owned by possession alone without a written title. It was and is free of all burdens, of services or periodical payments. Its origins can be traced to the occupation of the islands by the Norse.

Ultimus Haeres.—This Latin tag is used in connection with the law of succession and refers to the rule of law that the Crown (State) succeeds to the property or estate of any person who dies intestate and leaves no relatives who can succeed to it. It is the duty of any person who has any of such property in his possession to account for it to the representative of the Crown appointed for the purpose.

Ultra vires.—This Latin phrase is much used by lawyers. Roughly translated it means "beyond the powers of" and the doctrine of *ultra vires* is of importance in many fields of law, usually in relation to bodies who are created by or under statute but not to natural persons. Only a few can be mentioned. A company's objects, set out in its memorandum of association, limit its powers and anything the company does outwith the scope of its objects is *ultra vires*. The same is true of any corporation (companies are indeed a particular kind of corporation). A Secretary of State or other government minister on whom power to make regulations, orders or rules for certain purposes specified in a statute is conferred, has to ensure that all the provisions he makes in the regulations, orders and rules come within the powers so conferred. It follows that if any provision is outwith these powers it is *ultra vires* and the courts may declare the provision to be so. Local authorities on whom power is conferred by statute to make by-laws must also avoid including an *ultra vires* provision in them. If an arbiter in his award deals with any matter that has not been referred to him in the submission he is acting *ultra vires*. If a mandatory's (see **Mandate**) act is not within the powers conferred on him by the mandate it is *ultra vires*. A trade union which takes any action outwith the powers conferred on it by statute or by its own rules also acts *ultra vires*. A natural person, however, can never act *ultra vires* in his own affairs. So long as he complies with the law in general he is within his powers.

United Kingdom.—Scotland, England and Wales and Northern Ireland comprise the United Kingdom.

Urine test.—This phrase derives from the wording of the Road Traffic Act 1972. The Act provides for the taking and testing of a sample of urine obtained in the same circumstances and for the same purpose as a **blood test**. The first sample of urine is disregarded. The equivalent to the blood/alcohol limit is 107 mg. of alcohol in 100ml. of urine.

Ut intus.—Simply "as within". A reference in one part of a document or a book, perhaps, to some statement in another part of the same document or book.

V

Vassal.—This word derives from the feudal law of Scotland which formerly governed all rights in heritable property. Originally rights in land were given off gratuitously by the owner under conditions of fealty and military service to be performed to the granter by the receiver, the radical right remaining to the granter. Feus, however, ceased to be gratuitous and became the subject of commerce, services of a civil or religious kind being substituted for military. Later still the receiver was granted a **feu** charter by the owner and was taken bound to pay a feuduty in cash. Over the centuries there have been many changes.

Nowadays feu charters are still granted and contain conditions about the use to which the land feued can be put, and other provisions about title, warranty and writs. But legislation now prohibits the imposition, or payment, of any feuduty or performance of any other service by the purchaser or feuar for the benefit of the **superior** or granter. What have remained the same, however, are theoretically the relationship between and the names given to the granter — he is still known as the superior — and to the receiver who is still known as the *vassal*. But these are names, and have no substance of the kind embodied in the dictionary definition of the word, which is one who holds lands from and renders homage to a superior. What the superior owns is the **superiority** or *dominium directum* of the land feued; the vassal owns the right of property or *dominium utile,* which includes possession, of the land.

Verdict.—A verdict is the judgment given after proceedings in a criminal court have reached their conclusion. Where the proceedings are summary or taken by a judge without a jury the verdict is given by the judge; where there is a jury the verdict is given by the jury.

The verdict may be one of three, namely:

(a) "guilty", which means that the accused person has been found by the judge, or, as the case may be, by the jury or a majority of the jury, to have committed the crime or offence with which he has been charged. The judge, either at once or after further inquiry (*e.g.* by way of "background reports"), passes sentence on the accused after the Crown has asked him to do so;

(b) "not guilty", which means that the judge, or the whole or a majority of the jury, has found that the accused did not commit the crime or offence. The judge discharges the accused; and

(c) "not proven" which means that the judge is, or the whole or a majority of the jury are, not satisfied that the prosecutor has proved that the accused committed the crime or offence with which he has been charged. The judge discharges the accused in this case also.

Veritas.—This Latin word gives expression to a ground of defence — the truth — in an action of damages for defamation. It is a complete defence to prove that the statement complained of in the action is true, the pursuer's case being that it is false. At common law the defender had to prove the truth of all material statements, justifying everything in the allegedly defamatory statement and thus meeting the whole substance of the complaint. Statutory provision has altered the position by providing that the plea will not fail merely because the defender has failed to prove the truth of words which do not materially injure the pursuer's reputation.

Vest, to.—When land or moveables, or rights in either, are said to "vest" in a person it means that the rights then become that person's property. He has a title to them; they belong to him.

Vexatious litigant.—Persons have in general free access to the civil courts to obtain redress of grievances, but a person who has raised or persisted in an action in the full knowledge that he had no ground for action, or has raised an action or taken decree in breach of an agreement not to do so, or has maliciously repeated what is substantially the same as a previous claim, may be regarded by the court as a "vexatious litigant" and be required to obtain a Lord Ordinary's authority to initiate a further action. The Lord Ordinary's decision is final.

Vicarious liability.—There is vicarious liability where one person may be sued and held liable for wrong actually committed by another, causing damage whether to persons or property. It is justified on a number of grounds but it may be said that the only real justification for it is the practical one that it is desirable to impose liability on a defender who is in a position to pay damages and who is normally insured against the risk. An employer is vicariously liable to third parties for injury or damage caused to them by the fault of his employee, acting in the course of his employment. Whether or not a person is an employee is a question of fact in each case. A corporation is also liable for the wrongdoing of its agents. "Agent" is interpreted widely for this purpose and covers many cases of acting for another in a matter in which the latter has an interest. The employer or corporation is liable whether the wrong was the result of an intentional act or of an act of negligence done within the scope of the agent's authority or the servant's employment. An employer is liable if the employee is employed under a contract of service (but not a contract for services) and so long as the act was done in the course of the employee's employment and was in breach of some duty owed to the injured person. The injured person may be a fellow employee. The agent or employee does not cease to be liable for the harmful consequence of his conduct. If the employer pays damages to the injured person he has a right of action against the agent or employee for the sum paid. But the right of action is seldom used, and even if used would infrequently result in reimbursement.

Violent profits.—Where a person is deprived of possession of lands — to possession of which he has a right — by another whether forcibly (*e.g.* a squatter) or without violence (as in the case of a tenant whose right to continue in occupation is in doubt), the person so deprived is entitled to bring an action of summary ejection of the intruder and to claim damages from him. The damages (or violent profits) are double the rent of certain houses and tenements, and, in rural subjects, are the greatest profit the pursuer could have derived from the land. They are not due if, and so long as, the defender possessed in good faith, or an issue of title to possess is before the courts.

Void.—A void transaction (*e.g.* a contract) is one which from the beginning has no legal existence or effect, produces no obligation and can be repudiated or ignored by either party without any ill consequences. Examples of void transactions are a contract of service providing restrictions on the spending of earnings, a hire-purchase contract in which any party agrees that a particular sheriff court will have power to determine questions arising out of it, and a marriage contracted between persons who are within the forbidden degree of relationship. A void transaction is frequently referred to as being null and void.

Voidable.—A voidable transaction is one which is valid and produces an obligation but contains a defect which entitles one of the parties to rescind it, or have it declared ineffective (*reduced*) by a court in which case it is treated as if it had never been constituted. An example is a contract into which one of the parties has been persuaded to enter by fraud, another is a marriage contracted by parties one of whom turns out to be impotent with the result that the marriage is never consummated. Impotence means not only physical incapacity for sexual intercourse but also invincible repugnance to and revulsion from intercourse with the other party to the marriage existing at, and continuously since, the date of the marriage. A petition for

112

declarator of nullity of marriage must be made to the Court of Session and a decree, if granted, declares authoritatively that the parties have never been married.

Volenti non fit injuria.—This Latin phrase gives expression to a principle of the Scots law of **reparation.** Broadly it means that a person who has been injured may be held to have known of and voluntarily accepted the risk of the harm which befell him and caused him the injury complained of. It does not apply in all circumstances. For it to apply it must be shown that the pursuer, freely and voluntarily with full knowledge of the nature and extent of the risk he ran, agreed expressly or impliedly to take it. It must not merely be some risk; it must be risk of the particular kind of harm which he suffered.

W

Waiver.—Waiver consists in the general sense of conduct by one party which implies acceptance of another party's conduct and the giving up of any claim to which the conduit would normally give rise. Thus where it is said that a party "waives" a claim or waives an objection, it means that he does not make the claim or renounces the objection.

It has a rather special use in the context of heritable property. Where land is held subject to feudal conditions, one of which may be for instance that the building constructed on the land is to be used only as a dwellinghouse, the owner of the building may ask the feudal superior to grant him a waiver of the condition to enable him to use the building e.g. as a shop or an office. Such a change in conditions can be effected by the superior granting a waiver. The Lands Tribunal for Scotland are now empowered by statute to alter such a condition and planning law has to be remembered in connection with a change of land use: see the Lands Tribunal Act 1949 as amended in 1963 and 1970.

Ward.—A **pupil** must have a **tutor** to act on his behalf in legal matters, a **minor** should for all practical purposes have a **curator** to assist him in these matters and a person of unsound mind must also have a curator if it is necessary for legal steps to be taken on his behalf. The pupil, minor or insane person may be referred to as the ward of the tutor or curator as the case may be. Other persons in need of care or guardianship may also be so referred to.

Warrant sale.—After a creditor has obtained a decree from the sheriff finding that his debtor owes him a sum of money, he is still faced with the problem of obtaining payment. One method of proceeding is for a copy of the **decree** to be served on the debtor accompanied by a letter requiring him to pay the debt, together with expenses of the action, within the number of prescribed days (between 6 and 15) appropriate in the particular case. This is performed by a sheriff officer and is known as a "charge of payment". If the debtor does not then pay (in most cases he does) the sheriff officer returns after the days of charge have expired (no specific period for return is prescribed) along with two appraisers (one in a summary cause) who prepare an inventory of articles belonging to the debtor which are worth as much as the amount of the debt, plus the expenses. A copy of the inventory is given to the debtor. The goods are then said to have been **poinded** and are held to be at the disposal of the creditor. The sheriff officer three times thereafter offers to sell the goods to the debtor at the value fixed by the appraisers. Not all articles belonging to the debtor can be poinded. Tools of trade, necessary clothing, beds and bedding, tables, chairs and heaters, for instance, cannot be. If the debtor does not thereafter settle the debt, the sheriff officer, if so instructed obtains a warrant from the sheriff authorising the sale of the articles poinded. The sale is advertised and must take place not less than eight and not more than 28 days after advertisement. It may, and frequently does, take place in the debtor's house and is conducted by an auctioneer under the supervision of the sheriff officer. The expression "warrant sale" is short for "warrant of sale".

Warranty.—A stipulation in a **contract** which is fundamental to it and for non-implement of which the contract can be annulled and **damages** claimed, is a warranty. Under the Sale of Goods Act 1979, a consolidating measure, it is provided a warranty is a stipulation collateral to the main purpose of the contract, breach of which gives rise to a claim for damages but not to a right to treat the contract as repudiated. This gives effect to English Law and, as Scots Law differs, the Act further provides that as regards Scotland "failure to perform a material part of the contract" of sale is a breach of contract. In Scotland therefore it is not of much importance whether a provision express or implied is called a stipulation, a condition or a warranty; the question is whether failure to implement it is a fundamental or material breach or a less important breach. If there is a failure to perform a material part of a contract of sale, the buyer is entitled within a reasonable time after delivery to reject the goods or to retain the goods and claim compensation or damages. The implied conditions in such a contract are to be found in ss. 12, 13 and 14 of the Act. Where the goods are specified or ascertained the right of property in them is transferred to the buyer when the parties intend it to be transferred and until that right of property is transferred, no question of breach of warranty can, of course, arise. There are rules for ascertaining the intention of parties, and the Act contains many other provisions about, for example, the right of disposal of goods sold, the risk of loss, deterioration or destruction of them, the transfer of title, the performance of the contract, the rights of an unpaid seller against the goods and actions for breach of contract. Special kinds of sale, *e.g.* **auction sales, credit sales** and sales **C.I.F.** and **F.O.B.** are also dealt with. All these provisions have given rise to dispute. The subject is a difficult one, the difficulties being added to by the fact that "warranty" when used in relation to goods manufactured in England has, so far as the manufacturer is concerned, its English meaning. It should be mentioned that hire purchase, credit sales or conditional sales of moveable property have additional rather than different provisions applicable to them. A contract of hire purchase (and other similar credit sales) is not, of course, a true contract of sale. It is a contract of hire and only when all the instalments of hire have been paid does the right of property pass. The Consumer Credit Act 1974 should be looked at.

Wayleave.—A wayleave is a development of the right conferred by a **servitude**. Its purpose is to enable land to be used for a purpose benefiting persons other than the owner of the land. Examples are a right to run a pipeline through land or electricity cables and pylons or telephone lines over it. This differs from a servitude in there being no **dominant tenement**.

Whitsun or **Whitsunday.**—Whitsunday is the seventh Sunday after Easter and is the term day in Scotland on which a tenant whose tenancy begins on Whitsunday may be called on to remove from premises let to him. For most legal purposes Whitsunday is fixed as 15 May, but s. 4 of the Removal Terms (Scotland) Act 1886 provides that entry to or removal from a tenanted house shall take place on 28 May (or on the following day if the 28 be a Sunday).

Will.—The law of wills is complex although, over the years, it has become easier for a valid will to be made. This note deals only with the fringes of the subject the purpose of making a will and the effect on a will of the subsequent marriage of the testator (the man or woman who made the will) or the birth of his or her child. In using the word "will" it has to be borne in mind that in addition to the short, simple type of will there are also testamentary writings of a much more complex kind — a trust disposition and settlement creates a trust, a last will and testament may have elaborate provisions about say, children, grandchildren, legacies of money and specific legacies (*e.g.* of jewellery).

All wills are, however, made by a person to take effect on his death and are concerned with the disposal of property belonging to him, or disposable of by him, at the date of his death. Whatever a will contains by way of bequests, it cannot, of course, deprive a surviving spouse of his *jus relicti* or her *jus relictae* or children of their **legitim.** Thus a testator may bequeath to persons other than his widow and children, his heritable property and, if there are children as well as a widow, one-third of his moveable property or, if there are no children, one-half. If he leaves neither widow nor children he can dispose by will of all he owns. Any person of sound mind and whether of full age or a **minor** (though not a **pupil**) has capacity to make a will. Even if it is of no concern to the owner of properties or goods who is to become the owner of them after his death he should nonetheless make a will to ensure that there will be executors (see **Executor**) to be responsible for the winding up of the estate and if, for instance, the testator is a parent with more than one child, to avoid dispute amongst the children about succession to heirlooms and other valuables. It should identify clearly the maker and the beneficiaries, it should include a clause disposing of the **residue** and it should revoke all prior wills. It must also be validly executed, *i.e.* it should be signed and, unless **holograph** the signature of the testator witnessed.

A will must be in writing, type or print though not in a particular

115

form. A **holograph** will is effective so long as it is wholly written and signed by the testator, no witnesses being then required. A will in printed form completed in writing is valid if signed before witnesses or "adopted as holograph" by the testator adding those words to it in his own hand and signing it.

Printed will-forms with blank spaces are not recommended for use in testamentary writings.

A will is not revoked by the marriage of the testator after it is made but may be presumed to be revoked by the subsequent birth of a child. Only the child can seek to have the will revoked and the question whether a will is or is not revoked in the last-mentioned case depends on the circumstances of each case. A person who leaves a will when he dies is described as having died testate; a person who leaves no will dies intestate. If a will leaves part of the estate undisposed of, the testator is described as having died partially testate (or intestate).

Witness.—A person who, on oath or solemn affirmation, gives evidence in an action. Less technically, any person who gives information to another about a matter in which the other has a proper interest.

Witness summons.—This is a colloquial term for **citation** of a witness. No person has a duty to attend at court as a witness unless he has been formally cited to do so. The form of citation requires that the witness be notified of the names of the pursuer and defender in the action and of the place and date where his attendance is required. It must also specify the time, not being less than 48 hours, at which he is required to be available in court to give evidence. A witness so cited and who, after being given sufficient cash to meet his travelling expenses, if any, fails to attend may be penalised. The citation is dated and signed by a sheriff officer or the solicitor of the party citing the witness.

Young offender.—This term is used in relation to a young person over 16 and under 21 years of age who has been found guilty of an offence or a crime. It is not competent for such a person to be sent to prison, but instead the court may sentence him or her to a period of detention, but may do so only if they are of opinion that no other method of dealing with him or her is appropriate. The period must not exceed that for which the offender could be sent to prison had that been competent. Sections 44 and 45 of and Schedule 5 to the Criminal Justice (Scotland) Act 1980 are the most recent and comprehensive provisions on the matter, but other earlier Acts contain lesser provisions. Children under 16 years of age who have or are alleged to have committed offences are provided for by the Children and Young Persons (Scotland) Act 1937, as amended by the Social Work (Scotland) Act 1968 and the said 1980 Act. The 1968 Act itself, as amended by the 1980 Act, also contains extensive provisions about children including, in particular, provisions about children's hearings and reporters mentioned earlier in this glossary.